See Me Naked

See Me Naked

~

Black Women Defining Pleasure in the Interwar Era

TARA T. GREEN

Rutgers University Press

New Brunswick, Camden, and Newark, New Jersey, and London

LCCN 2021015661
A British Cataloging-in-Publication record for this book is available
from the British Library.

References to internet websites (URLs) were accurate at the time of writing. Neither
the author nor Rutgers University Press is responsible for URLs that may have
expired or changed since the manuscript was prepared.

⊖ The paper used in this publication meets the requirements of the
American National Standard for Information Sciences—Permanence
of Paper for Printed Library Materials, ANSI Z39.48-1992.

www.rutgersuniversitypress.org

Manufactured in the United States of America

Contents

Illustrations follow page 110.

See Me Naked

Introduction

Pleasure Is All Mine

"The water! Luxurious, voluptuous, lovely. Lapping, caressing, loving my bare body—when I get way out and slip my bathing suit down and no one can see me naked."[1] Alice Dunbar-Nelson described a naturally satisfying, intimate moment of pleasure in the private space of her diary. Using the pen to express the exhilaration of this most personal experience—her flesh in tune with the titillating sense of touch brought on by the "caressing" of a liquid body—she enjoys being overtaken with "bare" ecstasy that calls to her to surrender. Hidden away from public scrutiny is where a Black woman who cherished respectability joyfully reminisces about her indulgence of feelings that she wishes not to forget.

For Dunbar-Nelson, as with so many of her Black sisters of the early twentieth century, publicly indulging pleasure may have caused a conflict with respectability. Indeed, the enjoyment of pleasure, as Dunbar-Nelson describes, was to be tempered in public spaces, hidden where no one "can see me naked." Covering up would be a means by which the race may be advanced, maybe. According to Evelyn Brooks-Higginbotham, respectability politics was a method employed by African American women in the late nineteenth century, and it "equated public behavior with individual self-respect and with the advancement of African Americans as a group."[2] African American Christian women, especially those of the emerging middle class, "felt certain that 'respectable' behavior in public would earn their people a measure of esteem from white America, and hence they strove to win the black lower class's psychological allegiance to temperance, industriousness, thrift, refined manners, and Victorian sexual morals."[3] At minimum, Brooks-Higginbotham describes a public performance, a kind of masking, that Black women felt would lead to meeting a standard. Whether that standard was self-imposed by Black folks or perceived as necessary to become equal to Whites is debatable. Yet, expectations of respectability had an impact on how the women saw themselves and each other. Their adherence to respectable performance also shows that they knew they *were seen*, that they were the objects of voyeurs; therefore, respectability was their way of influencing how people analyzed and judged their bodies and from that scrutiny made decisions about their societal worth. Looking at respectability politics as "one of the earliest theorizations of gender" by members of the National Association of Colored Women (NACW), which was founded by Black women in 1896, Brittney Cooper argues that the women "imposed a respectability requirement on those women who would become educators of public opinion, in part because the work required an intrinsic placing of the Black female body on display for white consumption."[4] Though there is most certainly contradictions in the practice and theory, more specifically, that in order to define the self's behavior it is done with the oppressor in mind, there is no denying the fact that there is an act in process and that the act has a purpose.

Appearing respectable requires a series of public acts that are performed for the good of the Black masses. Although Brooks-Higginbotham is speaking of the generation of African American women who were born after emancipation (1865), the respectable practices resonated for generations. And, may still. In his study of contemporary popular Black women, Shayne Lee observes, "With overt attempts to downplay sexuality, black women resist negative images and sexual stereotypes in an attempt to secure respectability and empowerment for all black Americans."[5] Lee is referring to stereotypes that Patricia Hill Collins and other Black feminist scholars have noted were designed as "controlling images." Two of those figures that were prominent during the interwar era as holdovers from the slavery era are the mammy and jezebel figures. Mammy, known as a fat, Black, and undesirable, woman did not pose a sexual threat. Collins notes, "The mammy image buttresses the ideology of the cult of true womanhood, one in which sexuality and fertility are severed. 'Good' White mothers are expected to deny their female sexuality. In contrast, the mammy image is one of an asexual woman."[6]

A second idea about Black women looks at them as incapable of being associated with respectability as they publicly flaunted their sexuality. These jezebels were sexually lascivious. An image that was popular during slavery, a proclaimed owner of her enslaved body could not help but be enticed by her sexuality. This was especially true for Black women with light skin. Their skin color heightened their attractiveness and sexual allure, making them even more irresistible. According to Collins, "the jezebel, whore, or hoochie is central in the nexus of controlling images of Black womanhood. Because of efforts to control Black women's oppression, historical jezebels and contemporary 'hoochies' represent a deviant Black female sexuality."[7] Jezebel figures were still prominent in the American consciousness during the interwar era. As I will discuss, we find that some strategically embodied the jezebel in their public performances, especially in film. It is, then, the imposition of the limiting stereotypes that Black women resisted, especially in public performances.

In resistance to these one-dimensional representations of Black women that were largely contrived by White perspectives, Black women used their bodies to counter public opinions about them even if the public continued to believe the stereotypes. There is a sacrifice in these acts. As they speak, as they move, bodies tell stories, but the meaning of the stories is not always heard. In her overview of studies dedicated to Black women's sexuality, Michelle Michell finds, "The notion that African-American women developed a code of silence around intimate matters as a response to discursive and literal attacks on black sexuality has influenced studies of turn-of-the-century club women, reformers, and workers ever since Darlene Clark Hine in 1989 labeled this practice the 'culture of dissemblance.'"[8] Dissemblance refers to Black women asserting control of their bodies by "protecting their inner lives and selves," a response to being considered jezebel figures worthy of or welcoming rape.[9] In conversation with Mitchell, L. H. Stallings asserts, "In regards to gender and sexuality then, dissemblance and silence allows a policing of sexuality that is supported through social and political rhetoric of a group of people. In response to this politics of sexuality in African America, Black women could be rescued by their Black men or ideologically stoned with the markers of Jezebel, Sapphire, or Mammy."[10] Black women have used their bodies to re-center and resist beliefs about them. In their resistance, we may ask, When the fullness of a Black woman's body is ignored, what happens to the power of the body? If the body is disempowered by the silencing of its story, is it possible to recover the body's narrative?

I proceed from the belief that respectability practice represses the desires of the Black female body and its relationship to the woman's mind and spirit. Though I also agree with scholars of early twentieth-century Black women's studies that there are merits of respectability as an activist practice, this does not mean that, as Farah Jasmine Griffin observes, "Such a politics leaves little room for those who choose not to conform."[11] Respectability offers a covering up of the nakedness—a woman's vulnerability, her true nature, and her pleasurable desires. Extrapolating from an archive of various kinds of performances and resistance practices, this study is concerned with uncovering how Black women, fully aware of respectability requirements, made personal and strategic decisions to pursue pleasure during the interwar period (1919–1938) despite the expectations.

Defining Pleasure

Defining pleasure is an act of free discovery. For Black women, indulging in pleasure is an undeniable expression of their choice to explore rather than silence their bodies' desires. Pleasure is derived from *plaisir*, an Old French word meaning to please.[12] Michael Nylan observes that *pleasure* is the only English word "capacious enough to allow for the complex bodily processes supposedly registered in the senses, emotions, heart, and mind."[13] Further, in her study of pornography, Black feminist scholar Jennifer Nash identifies various "ecstatic pleasures . . . pleasures in looking, pleasures in being looked at, pleasures in performing racial fictions, pleasures in upending racial fictions . . . pleasures which are both deeply personal (aesthetic, erotic, sexual) and deeply social, and that form the basis of political communities and identities."[14] In other words, pleasure is a full-bodied experience, both literally and figuratively. It allows for a level of satisfaction from an external experience that meets mental and physical desires of the body.

There is no single or absolute way of thinking about pleasure. According to psychologist Paul Bloom, it's complicated: "The depth of pleasure is hidden from us. People insist that the pleasure that they get from wine is due to its taste and smell, or that music is pleasurable because of its sound, or that a movie is worth watching because of what's on the screen. And of course this is all true . . . but only partially true. In each of these cases, the pleasure is affected by deeper factors, including what the person thinks about the true essence of what he or she is getting pleasure from."[15]

Both Bloom and Nash speak to the multiplicity of pleasures that reach deep into the source of "true essence." I too see the multiple complex contours of pleasure. More specifically, this work will explore the aspects as an intense feeling of satisfaction, the identified sources of enjoyment, and the forms of escape that may be derived from an activity such as singing, acting, writing, or sex. Such enjoyable experiences, I argue, are acutely private and unapologetic, but may be experienced in public or not, and might be shared with another, or not. *See Me Naked* looks at the significance of multiple, layered meanings of pleasure to Black women during the interwar era, a time when pleasurable acts were heavily weighted against the good of the advancement of the people. Inspired by their archives (e.g., their music, stage performances, personal writings, interviews), I found women who performed to both cover and reveal who they were as Black women. It is there, in the archives, that I looked for the places where the women revealed how pleasure existed beyond the norms of expectations. Ultimately, *See Me Naked* asks, How have Black women dared to expose inner parts of themselves to define pleasure on their own terms?

For our purposes, I advance a central guiding idea that pleasure is for the self. It is, as a young Black transwoman shared with me about her coming out, "The most selfish thing I have ever done."[16] When Black women embrace pleasure, they do not see it as a decision or an act that they engage to advance their community. Although others may benefit from a Black woman's pleasure, it is a pursuit that is about fulfilling the desires of the woman first and foremost. The others may include members of the race, audience members, allies, friends, lovers, voyeurs, and anyone who encounters the Black woman at the time she is enjoying her time of pleasure for the self. Advocating for the indulgence and exploration of pleasure, adrienne maree brown states, "I have seen how denying our full, complex selves—denying our aliveness and our needs as living, sensual beings—increases the chance that we will be at odds with ourselves, our loved ones, our coworkers and our neighbors on this planet."[17] As a self-indulgence, pleasure can empower Black women and provide them with the tools needed to survive in hostile environments, a world that teaches her to be at odds with her body, a world that attempts to deny her the ability to choose when and how she can enjoy happiness. Black women in states of pleasure resist these and any such attempts. And, in fact, when a Black woman puts enjoying pleasure first, she may leave a loved one disappointed by the act.

To be sure, pleasure is what taps into personal enjoyment, whatever way that is defined by the woman. However, it is not any action that leads to imbalance or harm to the self or others. As brown clarifies, it is not "excess," such as the idea that money can bring happiness and take away other kinds of feelings.[18] Enjoying pleasure is not being "in a state of ecstasy at all times, but rather to learn how to sense when something is good for you."[19] Yet, it is possible to strive for and live a life that is pleasurable. That is to say, a major aspect of the woman's life is pleasurable, for it is an action or a series of actions that brings incomparable joy. For Black women, this becomes especially important. Pursuing pleasure gives a Black woman autonomy over the self and gives her an opportunity to learn more about who that self is irrespective of public scrutiny and community expectations.

As I see it primarily concerned with the self, pleasure, then, is not to be confused with the erotic. Audre Lorde's concept of the erotic is well known in Black women's sexuality studies; therefore, I will use it as a guide to delineate the primary difference. Although the erotic is closely related to sexual desire, as she explains, "it is not just sexual desire; it is also a measure between the beginnings of our sense of self and the chaos of our strongest feelings. It is an eternal sense of satisfaction to which, once we have experienced it, we know we can aspire. For having experienced the fullness of this depth of feeling and recognized its power, in honor and self-respect[,] we can require no less of ourselves."[20] It also involves enjoyment of work: "For once we begin to feel deeply about all aspects of our lives, we begin to demand from ourselves and from our life pursuits that they feel in accordance with that joy which we know ourselves to be capable of."[21] Lorde's characteristics of the erotic as "a source of power," "a sense of satisfaction and completion," and "personifying creative power and harmony" are closely aligned with pleasure.[22] There is one important difference: I do not see pleasure as connected to "sharing," which for Lorde is the first function of the erotic. She observes, it provides "the power which comes from sharing deeply any pursuit with another person."[23] As in the case of Dunbar-Nelson's pleasurable engagement with water as a singular act, pleasure is an individual experience that does not depend on anyone else to be empowering or joyful. I am not dismissing the possibility of activism as a pleasurable action that advanced communities, but I am illuminating the ways in which Black women sought and claimed something that was specifically theirs, no matter the costs. I think here about Alice

Dunbar-Nelson, a suffragist and civil rights activist, who found pleasure in writing a diary where she described traveling to a speaking engagement and taking the time to walk in a park. She also enjoyed the sexual pleasure of women and men when she traveled despite the fact that she was married. Dunbar-Nelson's choices show how one woman escaped the pressures of life by engaging in a multiplicity of pleasures.[24]

As seen in the Black women's lives and experiences I discuss in this book, at times for Black women pleasure is exercised in the transformative act of movement. Movement—of the body from one position to another as in dance, from one location to another as in traveling—becomes a means by which to express the self in a deliberate language of resistance. Within the self is where pleasurable acts form and movement speaks *of* the self as it speaks *from* the self. For Black women, pleasure in movement may be enacted as a reaction to a threat of suppressed creativity. As pleasure is equated with freedom, movement away from oppression becomes necessary to save the self from the threat and to pursue opportunities. Historically, southern spaces such as segregated spaces required strategic kinds of movement; those movements were intentional navigational acts for the purpose of surviving within restrictive boundaries. Even if the Black girl or woman decided to remove herself from the South or any other part of the United States to escape restrictions or dangerous settings, there would have been an immeasurable form of pleasure in this movement, for it was an act that satisfied the self's need to be free.

To escape the oppression and suppression of segregation, Black women searched for pleasure in freedom in France. In her comprehensive study *Bricktop's Paris: African American Women in Paris between the Two World Wars*, Tracy Sharpley-Whiting delves into the lives of African American women performers, writers, activists, and artists who took up residency in France during the interwar period. There, many of the women were welcomed by Ada "Bricktop" Smith, born in New York in 1922, who became "a fifteen-year resident of Paris."[25] Through her "various eponymous clubs" she "provided a space where she served as both the anchor and the magnet for the expatriate community of African American women."[26] Some of these women included Jessie Fauset, Laura Wheeler, Eslanda Goode Robeson, Josephine Baker, Ethel Waters, and Alberta Hunter. Smith's communal space provided safety for women who were traveling alone as well as other much-needed resources and support.

This was a diverse group of women from different parts of the United States who wanted an experience that was not bound by the conventions of African American respectability and American racism. They were heterosexual and bisexual. Sharpley-Whiting captures what might be seen as the need to pursue pleasure during this period: "In America, black women were corseted, policed— and policed one another and themselves. In Paris, freedom was creative, social, and sexual."[27] Of Baker, in particular, Sharpley-Whiting concludes, "No one made greater use of the latter in Paris than Josephine Baker."[28] These negotiations of the foreign landscape did not shield them from the complexities of race, nationality, and gender. As Sharpley-Whiting notes, "Though they were talented, they were also privileged as Americans and exoticized as blacks."[29] They too were subject to the scrutiny of voyeurs, but, like the women I discuss in the chapters that follow, they leveraged the attention given to them to advance their professional careers and personal desires.

As Josephine Baker and other entertainers would show, there is pleasure in artistic performance. Public performative acts can be favorable to the performer of an action of movement as well as to the observer. Erin Chapman argues that Black women of the New Negro era "were not simply objectified by the sex-race marketplace but participated in it on many levels."[30] As a form of entertainment, there is a oneness that is likely to occur between the artist and the act, whereas the act itself allows for the body to transcend and move beyond the act. Chapman observes, "The sex-race marketplace would prove to be a simultaneously liberating and constricting space, one through which black women played a part in the formulation and dissemination of modern subjectivities and ideals of femininity and were also consumed as racialized, dehumanized objects of desire."[31] Observers hear this moment in the pitch of a finely tuned voice, see it in the female performer's eyes, or feel it in her smile or facial expression. Bloom argues that performance is assessed as a pleasure by "the perceived amount of effort." He goes on, "Effort matters as well for how much we value our own creations."[32] That expression of emotion is a shared act and the personal becomes infectious in the public sphere. Yet, this cannot be confused with the deliberate act of respectability, for this choice of pleasure through performance is to satisfy the self; if others are pleased, their pleasure is second to the pleasure of the performer.

Black Women, Pleasure, and Sex

Pleasure is often equated with sex. For Black women during the interwar era, sex could intersect with pain, trauma, and fear. Pleasure is private not simply because of the history that has required silence for a sense of survival but also because of the space needed for Black women's pleasure to occupy. Thus, a body in the state of pleasure is a body that is experiencing the intersection between resistance, a measure of satisfaction, and freedom.

Returning to the experience described by Dunbar-Nelson, we must consider the significance of touch in achieving sexual pleasure. Touch may include a series of external, wanted, welcomed movements that are shared with another or experienced alone with the self. Pleasure as a full-bodied experience, then, is the absorption of feelings that simultaneously satisfies the body and mind. Indeed, pleasurable touch involves a consensual interaction where there is a lack of control and also a feeling of self-empowerment. What the body feels and the mind processes is a feeling that can be both fulfilling and overwhelming, and it is not likely to be paralleled by any other experience at a different time.

To enjoy sexual pleasure is to embark on a transformative experience that may not be translatable in spoken language. It causes the body itself to speak—one cell to another, one movement to another, one thought to another. Further, such a transformative, illegible experience suggests that the person enjoying the interaction at a specific time is, at least for that time, not the same person she was before the experience began and may not be at the climax or end of the experience. Brought into a new kind of knowledge about her own body and its relationship to an external stimulant, a woman can exercise her agency and by doing so can achieve a level of freedom that is intensely and uniquely personal.

Challenges to Black Women's Pleasure

African American women's public history with sex intersects with pain and trauma. Choice is often negotiated between what must be and what is. One of the most famous examples of this is Harriet Jacobs's *Incidents in the Life of a Slave Girl* where she describes the sexual advances of her "owner," Dr. Flint, who was known to engage in unwanted sexual relationships with his "slave girls" and then sell them away from their families when he chose to do so. She writes about her choice to fend off Dr. Flint, a move that was an act of resistance to his intent to enjoy her teenaged body. Telling, too, as in writing, is an act of resistance. Writing, as it performs for the public, may also mask a level of the interiority, which Joan Morgan has appropriately identified as "the quiet composite of mental, spiritual and psychological expression."[33] Jacobs's narrative relies on the narrative of respectability to explain her decision to choose Mr. Sands to father her children rather than to allow herself to be coerced into rape. Within the boundaries of slavery, we find that there is a tension between the public and the private that leaves space for Black women's silence.

As a writer, she maneuvered within the boundaries of silence that still managed to reveal how her right to consent to pleasure in slavery was restricted and suppressed by Flint. Jacobs writes of a Black man that she wanted to marry, but the request was denied. Pleasure, therefore, is found in the act of resistance in the writing, hiding, and later escaping, for if she found any pleasure with Mr. Sands, and it is very possible that she did, her White female audience would certainly not allow her the right to share any feelings or emotions she had for the White man. The availability of Jacobs's life story speaks to the impact of generational violation. Morgan observes, "We've been considerably less successful, however, moving past that damage to claim pleasure and a healthy erotic as fundamental rights."[34] Silence empowers a system dependent on disempowerment and it enables violations of Black women's bodies.

If Black women and girls were not safe on plantations, they were not safe in the decades following emancipation. To provide safety would mean acknowledging their humanity. Saidiya Hartman notes, "In 1883, the age of consent was ten."[35] But what did this mean for "colored girls" who "were always presumed to be immoral"?[36] Consent was not required for those who chose the immoral. As more Black women moved from the South to the North, Black women organizers put measures in place to protect the newcomers from being taken into prostitution by men who waited for naive Black southern girls at ship docks and train stations. Unfortunately, for those who wanted to enjoy the pleasures of sex, they "risked harassment, arrest, and confinement."[37] Hartman goes on, "All colored women were vulnerable to being seized at random by the police; those who worked late hours, or returned home after the saloon closed or the lights were extinguished at the dance hall, might be arrested and charged with soliciting. If she had a sexually transmitted disease or children outside of wedlock or mixed-children, her conviction was nearly guaranteed."[38] In other words, freedom did not guarantee a right to pleasure.

Silence can be found in the archive as Hartman discovered when she sought "photographs exemplary of the beauty and possibility cultivated in the lives of ordinary black girls and young women and that stoked dreams of what might be possible if you could escape the house of bondage."[39] Finding none, she would have to rely on other kinds of archival records to imagine some of these lost vestiges of pleasure that photographers might have captured—"love in doorways" or hallways where "the first tongue kiss" occurred. To protect themselves from having their pleasure put on display or being seen physically or symbolically naked, Hartman surmises that "they refused the terms of visibility imposed on them" and "eluded the frame."[40] This is what it means to be both seen and unseen, to be both powerful and disempowered. Theirs is an ordinary, everyday performance of resistance.

Yet, Black people's writing during the interwar era, like the elusive photos, imprisons sexual desires. In his 1926 essay "Criteria of Negro Art," W.E.B. Du Bois questioned the absence of sex as an expression of shame in Negro Art. Du Bois was arguing for younger Black artists to not be bound by the expectations of Whites and the traditions of old. He proclaimed, "the young and slowly growing black public still wants its prophets almost equally unfree. We are bound by all sorts of customs that have come down as second-hand soul clothes of white patrons. We are ashamed of sex and we lower our eyes when people will talk of it. Our religion holds us in superstition. Our worst side has been so shamelessly emphasized that we are denying we have or ever had a worst side. In all sorts of ways we are hemmed in and our new young artists have got to fight their way to freedom."[41]

Du Bois saw avoiding the subject of sex in literature as keeping Black folks "unfree" or repressed as he simultaneously acknowledged that this is a "second-hand custom." Literary scholar Henry Louis Gates Jr., who says the essay was first presented as a speech "at the Chicago convention of the NAACP" in June 1926, quotes from this speech as evidence of his own observations about the silencing of sexual pleasures in African American literature during the period: "Though many will find this difficult to believe today, in a hip-hop era defined in part by graphic depictions of sexuality, sex was a taboo subject throughout much of the history of African-American literature. In fact, black authors, male and female, traditionally were downright prudish, avoiding black sexuality in their texts like the plague. (Cases of rape were an exception, seen as a sign of the brutality and psychosis of white oppression.) Reading classic black literature might lead one to conclude that black people abstained from having sex!"[42]

He goes on to point to the exceptions in literature, such as the women in Jean Toomer's *Cane*, a novel that Du Bois reviewed for its depiction of the "sexual lives of female characters."[43]

Literature taps into lived experiences and gives way to the imagination of the creator who attempts to convey the emotion of the experience to another. Claudia Tate delves into this in her seminal work, *Psychoanalysis and Black Novels: Desire and the Protocols of Race*, where she argues that Du Bois presents an "erotic relationship between art and propaganda" in the essay: "Du Bois seems unconsciously to associate propaganda for social reform with erotic desire. The eroticism is not depicted as mere sensuality; on the contrary, it is personified as a heroic ideal much like the noble and unobtainable queen of courtly romance to whom a knight would dedicate his chivalric zeal."[44] Tate is speaking to how the art as propaganda is an expression of psychological leanings and an expression of what is deeply personal. In the case of sex, moving beyond the politics of shame in the interwar era, especially for Black folks, was not so easily done. Ultimately, what New Negro artists' silence, Du Bois, Gates, and even Harriet Jacobs call attention to is the system of repression. In her study *Black Sexual Politics*, Patricia Hill Collins observes, "Sexual regulation occurs through repression, both by eliminating sexual alternatives and by shaping the public debates that do not exist. In order to prosper, systems of oppression must regulate sexuality, and they often do so by manufacturing ideologies that render some ideas commonsensical while obscuring others."[45] Black women have operated within such systems of oppression intent on addressing forms of regulation.

My purpose with this work is to explore (pun intended) the ways in which Black women of the interwar era navigated the treacherous terrain of respectability to claim pleasure as they made attempts to push past sexual regulations and the history of sexual violations as well as various forms of social and political restrictions. During the era, women received the right to vote (1920), but Blacks in the South would continue to fight for their rights until the 1965 Voting Rights Act was passed and signed. A constitutional ban on alcohol was in place from 1920 to 1933. The stock market crashed in 1929, sending the country into a major economic depression that lasted until the end of the decade. President

Franklin Roosevelt reacted with the New Deal, which provided government-supported programs for artists. The government also became vigilant of the spread of communism, prompting the First Red Scare, involving raids and arrests of suspected sympathizers. As the nation transitioned between wars, Black women exercised and expanded their rights as citizens. More specifically, as Treva Lindsey observes, Black women were particularly active in building communities and defining their own roles in society: "The activities of clubwomen, black suffragists, teachers in newly established 'Colored' schools, beauticians, and domestics, from the late nineteenth century until the mid-twentieth century, composed the New Negrohood experience" as these women engaged in politics, education and business.[46] In this current year, Black women continue the work that their ancestral activists began, reminding us that there is a very real link between the past and the present.

Black people of the interwar era were affected by these events as well as their bouts with racism. During this era, the grandchildren of the last generation of enslaved people were in the process of defining freedom in a society that held tightly to social and racial restrictions. How they were depicted in public spaces, such as film, theater, print media, literature, and how they represented themselves in these forms of media and in society shows a complex personal narrative that draws our attention to the tension between what was and what should be. Or, in other words, the tense relationship between public depictions and the private strivings of Black women.

Overlapping with this period is the New Negro era (1919–1940). Erin Chapman notes, "the New Negro era was not confined to any particular place, such as Harlem or Chicago, but was an aspect of the entire interwar fabric and its racial politics."[47] Alain Locke would describe it in "The New Negro" as an optimistic period in which,

the mind of the Negro seems suddenly to have slipped from under the tyranny of social intimidation and to be shaking off the psychology of imitation and implied inferiority. By shedding the old chrysalis of the Negro problem, we are achieving something like a spiritual emancipation. Until recently, lacking self-understanding, we have been almost as much of a problem to ourselves as we still are to others. But the decade that found us with a problem has left us with only a task. The multitude perhaps feels as yet only a strange relief and a new vague urge, but the thinking few know that in the reaction the vital inner grip of prejudice has been broken.[48]

Locke's proposal that the Negro "lacked self-understanding" and a movement toward "a strange relief and a new vague urge" is especially poignant for our purposes. He seems to point to the present moment as a time in which Black folks were consciously or subconsciously focusing on the inner self. It is here, in the midst of exploration, that I find Black women willing to publicly explore pleasure as a part of their identity. And not just to explore it but to find what kinds of pleasure made them who they were as individual members of the race for which Locke expressed such hope.

Perhaps Nella Larsen, with her depiction of New Negroes who appear stuck between the past and their present, tried to meet Du Bois's challenge when she published *Quicksand* in 1928 and *Passing* in 1929. How easy would it be for middle-class Black women, like Larsen who, according to Deborah McDowell, "wanted to tell the story of a black woman with sexual desires, but was constrained by a competing desire to establish black women as respectable in black middle-class terms"?[49] In her Black feminist analysis of Larsen's novellas, McDowell posits further that Larsen's novellas should be "examined through the prism of black female sexuality."[50] Larsen's *Passing* queries the tension between the Black middle class's sexual desires and the repression of those desires through the use of direct and indirect conversations and actions and establishes what McDowell sees as "taking more risks, calling more boldly into question the heterosexual priorities, maintained by the program of bourgeois uplift."[51] Told through the perspective of Irene, the protagonist, her observations, actions, and thoughts reveal the struggle she has as a married woman and being constrained by respectability. The rather reluctant conversation she has with her husband, Brian, who is a doctor, about their son Junior is a glaring example of the discomfort Irene has even discussing sex. She tentatively broaches the subject, "I'm terribly afraid he's picked up some queer ideas about things—some things—from the older boys, you know."

"Queer ideas?" he repeated. D'you mean ideas about sex, Irene?"
"Ye-es. Not quite nice ones. Dreadful jokes, and things like that." . . .
"Well what of it? If sex isn't a joke, what is it? And what is a joke?" . . .
"Exactly! And you're trying to make a molly-coddle out of him. Well, just let me tell you, I won't have it. And, you needn't think I'm going to let you change him to some nice kindergarten kind of school because he's getting a little necessary education. I won't! He'll stay right where he is. The sooner and the more he learns about sex, the better for him. And most certainly if he learns that it's a grand joke, the greatest in the world. It'll keep him from lots of disappointments later on."[52]

Setting aside the tension between Irene and Brian that, in part, has to do with Irene insisting that Brian be a doctor in America when he would rather live in Brazil, we see Larsen teasing out the relationship between freedom, gender, and sex. Brian and his son, as men, can express sexual desire or at least explore sexual curiosity when Irene, as a woman, cannot. Through Irene, Larsen speaks to the "casting down of eyes" that Du Bois calls young Black artists to avoid. Through Brian, Larsen dismisses the shame associated with sex. Junior, with his father's guidance, may be encouraged to not carry such shame, but Irene's identity as a middle-class woman gives her no such luxury.

Shame and sex are prevalent in the novel. Irene's attraction to Clare has been convincingly analyzed by McDowell who argues that "Larsen can flirt, if only obliquely, with the idea of a lesbian relationship between the two."[53] Irene's attraction to Clare is immediate. In seven paragraphs, Larsen writes how distracting Clare is to Irene and of the special attention Irene gives to Clare's mouth when she first sees Clare. She takes note of her "peculiar caressing smile," that she had a "wide mouth like a scarlet flower," and a smile that gave "a certain impression of assurance."[54] After giving a detailed description of the woman she did not initially recognize as Clare, she leaves her company thinking, "At that moment it seemed a dreadful thing to think of never seeing Clare Kendry again. Standing there under the appeal, the caress, of the eyes, Irene had the desire, the hope that the parting wouldn't be the last."[55] In her analysis of Irene's attraction to Clare, Elizabeth Dean observes, Irene's "queer desire and her urge to control optics of respectability are terminally incompatible."[56] Ultimately, Larsen uses her art to show how respectability suppressed sexual desire for middle-class Black women during this time as she also questions the possibility of women being the artists that Du Bois calls for if their personal experiences do not give them the opportunity to know how to maneuver around the shame.

Black Women in Film

Representations of sexuality in Black film during the interwar era expanded ideas that were teased and tested in literature. Oscar Micheaux's films tease out the relationship between race, skin color, and Black folks' pursuit of pleasure depicted as a search for a better life in the North. I would also see his Black characters' movement from the South to the North as an argument for their right to have pleasure. But, the restrictions of the early twentieth century, tightly held within Black communities, too often made pleasure pursuits a shameful act.

Responding to the mammy and jezebel figures, Micheaux's *Swing* (1938) is essentially a film that spotlights Black talent, but the main storyline focuses on three women from Alabama. Skin color determines categories, which determine experience with pleasure. Cora Smith is the "yellow hussy" who has an affair with

Mandy Jenkins's lover, Cornell. Cora has no job and this brings her much pleasure, as she enjoys being financially cared for by one man which frees her to enjoy a relationship with another man. After a fight between Mandy and Cora in an unnamed southern town, the film moves to New York City, where Cora has established a reputation as a star blues singer with a taste for alcohol. The only person who can keep her in line is a fist-swinging lover. She eventually breaks her leg and is replaced in the musical by the lovable Mandy who has also come to New York to work as a seamstress. Thanks to her adopted younger sister, Mandy not only gets the job but also successfully replaces Cora as the mammy character. To be sure, the light-skin mulatta or "hussy" is the unwanted villain in *Swing* who is tolerated by members of the performance community because she is talented and fits a certain expectation of the audience.

On film, both Cora and Mandy appear to be nearly the same shade of light brown, but they are in opposition to one another and this is established before they leave for New York. Mandy's position as a cook for White employers brings her respect as a member of a community of working women. Her sexuality is muted in favor of her identity as a laborer. Women in the southern community understand Mandy, for they too are in love with men whom they take care of. Understanding her "blues," they are also the ones who tell her the truth she does not want to hear—her man is driving around with a "stuck up hussy" in a car bought for her by another man. Mandy initially gives Cornell the benefit of the doubt because he is the source of her pleasure. What she will not admit is that Cornell is a no-good man who tells lies and tries to convince her that he is smarter than she. Mandy later admits that she loves the man—a man that hurt her so much she felt compelled to "wipe the floor" with another woman in a public place.

Cora is White, or "uppity." She is the mulatta figure, a daughter of the lascivious slave master and the jezebel. On one hand, Cora's light skin is attractive to the men and this gives her a privilege, at least among the men, that allows her to not worry about how she will care for her material needs or sexual desires. On the other hand, seeing, knowing that Cora lured the object of Mandy's plea-sure away, makes Cora destroyable. Destruction, pain, and trauma are the consequences of the "yellow hussy's" daring to dis-rupt the pleasure of a woman accepted in her community.

Pleasure has its limits for Micheaux's mulatta, but pain is abun-dant. Moving from being a "hussy" in Alabama to an "ornery woman" in New York only further marginalizes her from the Black community. A woman of noticeable height and girth, Cora is fully capable of hurting the stage manager, Sam, who she threatens to knock down. By the time she herself is punched by her dark-skin lover, the members of the cast seem satisfied that she has gotten what she deserves. Cora's scenes always place her opposite a man, usually one considerably darker than she. The jezebel's light flesh is punishable, a site for violence, the place where the trauma of the past clashes with the hope in the present. In three scenes, she sus-tains damage to her body. In the first instance, she is slapped by Mandy. Second, she is punched by her lover. The third time, she falls down the stairs and breaks her leg. No other character expe-riences violent injuries in the film. Why, then, is the mulatta wor-thy of injury, beatings, abuse, and trauma? According to Micheaux, a mulatta's flesh is malleable, resulting from a history of sexual shame. Her wounded flesh does not deserve or warrant lovable attention from anyone, for all have decided, long before she entered, that she is punishable.

Cora's flesh is further punished when she falls and breaks her leg and is unable to sing, opening the door for Mandy to take her place. Cora's fall is neither dainty nor graceful. As her intoxicated body slides and rolls down the stairs, she gives out a loud, shrill-ing scream that alerts the men in the bar that she is experiencing agony. They run to her rescue and see her light legs exposed above her thigh-high stockings. Her alluring sexuality is transformed into pronounced vulnerability among the men, and for the first time in this New York sequence, her pain is given attention as they whisk her away to Harlem Hospital. Cora's removal has the effect of silencing and satisfying the audience's need to suppress latent sexual desires. Finally, the audience is given the satisfaction of seeing her down, unthreatening, and sexually undesirable. Cora has been sufficiently dealt with for her offense of having been born, presumably, the daughter of a White man, and she is replaced with brown Mandy, whose status as servant makes her more worthy of being saved.

Micheaux uses Cora to play with two stereotypes. One character tells her why Cora s there: "This show can't get to first base without a blues singer in a mammy lead. They look for her in this type of show and Cora Smith is the best one in the whole Negro race." In fact, Cora is a misunderstood binary jezebel-mammy figure, both desirable and undesirable, deserving neither. Beyond her wounded body is her voice, the source of creative expression. Her worth is her voice. Although Micheaux treats her as a mulatta, or rather a jezebel figure, she is playing as a mammy, a figure known for being nonthreatening sexually. Her voice is separated from her body. Yet, her power is that she is fully aware that her voice is what gives her a position of value to the community that despises her, for Cora embodies the shame that causes castdown eyes.

Mandy is the preferred presence in the film. Always overlooked by men in favor of Cora, she leverages her relationship with a woman to advance her career. In fact, Man has been the one throughout the film who has had connections to women who do not feel intimidated by her but who feel as though they want to see her do well. It is a woman who tells her that her lover is cheating with Cora and it is a woman who gets her a job with the show and introduces her to the man who will be her next lover. Mandy's respectable behavior is rewarded. She does not pursue the man she ends up with but rather allows him to make advancements toward her.

Micheaux presents Mandy as a domestic who pretends to know how to sew, but this simply masks her ability to sing. As in a fairy tale, she is lifted from the position of service and elevated to the spotlight where the binary figure had been placed. In some ways, Micheaux illuminates the hidden—the Black woman in the shadows who is not seen for who she is and what she wants to do.

Mandy's ability to sing is what may carry her forward in society. It allows her movement and freedom from a place of domesticity, as it provides another way to have enjoyment that is hers. Though she can pretend to be someone else, a domestic mammy in this case, the fact that she has access to a place where pretending can happen gives her an opportunity to pursue a part of herself that is not dependent upon anyone other than herself. She owns her voice and the body from which the voice emanates.

I recognize here that a man provides her with the platform for the use of her voice. But they are codependents in this scenario. He will lose a substantial amount of money if Mandy does not agree to be the star. She also consents to being with him. For the first time in the film, she is not begging someone to see her, to acknowledge her, to give her respect. Her voice places her in a position of power as it did Cora, but in her case, her power does not intimidate the other Black people. This moment is hers. It is a moment of pleasure that has potential to last beyond the one show.

Why Pleasure Now?

Historical truths that challenge Black women's choices to pursue any form of pleasure have given way to scholarship on Black women's pleasure. Joan Morgan, in her essay "Why We Get Off: Moving Towards a Black Feminist Politics of Pleasure," illuminates the need for such a conversation. She observes that Patricia Hill Collins's *Black Feminist Thought* exemplified how "a great deal of energy has been spent disputing deeply entrenched and dehumanizing stereotypes—ranging from our uniquely mummified asexuality to our naturally animalistic, wanton and licentious ways."[57] Within this context of acknowledging the boorish treatment and castigation of Black women's bodies as objects, studies have thereby advanced "a mulish inattentiveness to black women's engagements with pleasure—the complex, messy, sticky, and even joyous negotiations of agency and desire that are irrevocably twinned in our pain," argues Morgan.[58] Pleasure, as she describes, was certainly a truth known to Black women of the interwar era.

Though Morgan is interested in looking at contemporary representations of Black women's pleasure, my work is concerned with establishing a genealogy by looking at representations of Black women in the interwar era and how those representations compel us to think of pleasure as an offspring of freedom; this becomes especially important when considering the connection between the South as a restricted space and the North as a place of hope. What did it mean for Black women of the era to have been legacies of a sexual and political history that may have been responsible for their very existence? How did they define themselves despite the call for respectability that Brooks-Higginbotham identifies as an activist lifestyle? How, in other words, did they at least attempt to move past the traumas associated with slavery? Collins informs us of the importance of pleasure, "In the context of a new racism, men and women who rescue and redefine sexuality as a source of power rooted in spirituality, expressiveness, and love can craft new understandings of Black masculinity and Black femininity needed for a progressive Black sexual politics. When reclaimed by individuals and groups, redefined ideas about sexuality and sexual practices can operate as sources of joy, pleasure, and empowerment that simultaneously affirm and transcend individual sexual pleasure for social good."[59] As respectability was important, I argue, so was reclamation. Despite their circumstances, Black women redefined who they were as sexual feminine beings.

Between 1918 and 1939, Black people moved in significant numbers from the South to the North and West seeking educational advancement, job opportunities, and safety from violence. In some cases, this would mean opportunities to pursue their artistic dreams as actors, singers, or musicians on stage or in movies, or it could mean attending colleges that were integrated and had adequate resources. Yet, as literature and studies of the era most certainly reveal, racism was prominent in all areas of the country and Black women had to navigate the sometimes dangerous terrain of trying to make a living in a society that defined them by their bodies. How, then, did Black women of the era resist perspectives that saw them as "invisible and hypervisualized"?[60]

My goal is to both recover and uncover pleasure as a central part of Black women's public and private lives. Furthermore, my intent in placing women of various backgrounds together provides the space to show how Black women's sexual desires are sometimes intertwined with their artistic expressions but certainly how those desires advance how they came to determine who they were as Black women. To achieve this, I look at aspects of private lives and public representations to form a narrative that counters perspectives that tend to see Black women's bodies as desexualized or hypersexualized objects. A Black woman, Zora Neale Hurston taps into the essence of the everyday pleasure of Black performance in "Characteristics of Negro Expression." Among other descriptions of Black expression, she sees "Will to Adorn," as a conscious action that "does not attempt to meet conventional standards, but it *satisfies the soul of its creator.*"[61] Hurston posits a theory of pleasure practice as interacting with expression by individual Black folks and among them, including those who are "acting out daily in a dozen streets in a thousand cities."[62] Black women see the acting of other Black women. Although there are many choices, I chose four women who had backgrounds that differ significantly from the other and whose contributions to society were equally as different. They were women who performed in various ways for a public audience of voyeurs. Whether it was as a paid stage performer, a socialite, or a teacher, these women had to define who they were—all of the selves of their being—and make it work for their good.

I chose well-known women to illuminate the voyeuristic practices enacted upon Black women and to consider how these women reacted to attempts to make them the objects of voyeurism subjected to respectability. In that voyeurism is the vulnerability that unacknowledged nakedness exposes—an experience the women dare to navigate, negotiate, resist, turnover, and do with as they will. Ironically, Langston Hughes, if not a public voyeur, was coincidently a fan and/or associate of each woman discussed in the chapters to come. His novel, *Not Without Laughter*, documents a perspective on how Black women were *seen* during the era. For our purposes, it serves as an adorned space to consider how Black women who found pleasure as performers tapped into their own sense of pleasure and defined themselves despite public scrutiny. I join Nash and other Black feminist scholars by "organizing around the paradoxes of pleasure rather than woundedness or the elisions of shared injury, around possibilities rather than pain."[63] Blues women singers, civil rights icons, comediennes were performers who were women—Black women who sought ways to look deeply within and push against the pressures without. In each chapter, I consider how their actions spoke a narrative dedicated to defining their Black female selves or, as Collins puts it, how "Black women's self-definitions of Black womanhood were designed to resist the negative controlling images of Black womanhood defined by Whites" and, I would add, at times, advanced by Black men.[64] To be sure, we find in these women's narratives wonderful, commendable expressions of self-love in ways that were gloriously selfish.

Chapter one looks at the life and representation of Nina Yolande Du Bois Williams, the only daughter and only surviving child of Dr. William E. B. Du Bois who was saddled with living within the Black elite's idea of respectability. Yolande, as she was called to distinguish her from the mother whose name she was given, is best known for marrying poet Countee Cullen in a lavish wedding. She has been, for the most part, seen in connection to men, namely her father, with whom she had a complicated relationship, as he was often absent and communicated with her largely by letters. These connections overshadow and silence what gave her pleasure. Du Bois Williams was a talented artist who enjoyed teaching. This chapter looks at the period of her life when she was an energetic, hopeful socialite at Fisk University and follows her as she found herself married and soon divorced from Cullen. More importantly, it uncovers her commitment to her teaching career. It ends with her last marriage to Arnette Franklin Williams and the birth of their daughter. In this chapter, I am interested in how a woman who was the daughter of a revered Black leader and intellectual strove to carve out an identity that was hers.

Chapter two focuses on the life and career of Lena Horne. Known as a sex symbol who came to be adored by civil rights activists, she developed a reputation for being able to sing, dance, and act. In her autobiography, *Lena*, Horne establishes herself as a respectable woman who pushed the limits of respectability. Further, Horne speaks rather frankly about the problems of silencing sexual desires and how this silencing proposes to act as a defense mechanism that covers shame and trauma among Black people. Horne's use of her body as a performer and as a scripted narrative subject gives voice to how she navigated an industry that favored light-skinned Black women. Moreover, she emphasizes how performance gave her access to pleasure.

Chapter three focuses on the career of the woman known as Moms Mabley, the most successful comedienne of her era, whose persona was known to brag of the attraction she had to younger men. Born Loretta Aiken in Brevard, North Carolina, she left to pursue a career as an entertainer at an early age. This chapter is drawn from a thin and spotty archive that makes an absolute timeline impossible, but Mabely most certainly built her career during the interwar era. It was during this time that she developed the character of Moms, a persona that expressed an attraction to young men. She gave pleasure to her audience as she enjoyed the pleasures of her public and private life. On the other hand, Mabley was also known to her colleagues as preferring relationships with women, which stood in stark contrast to her beloved Moms persona. Mabley persisted in her career and became increasingly popular from the interwar era through the civil rights movement. Mabley's long career speaks to her ability to confront and navigate boundaries as the country changed.

Chapter four looks at the blues from the perspective of the artist known as "Memphis Minnie." Born Lizzie Douglas, the phenomenal blues artist developed a reputation as a woman who could outplay blues men. As a guitar player and singer who began recording in the 1930s, Memphis Minnie saw herself as a legacy of Gertrude "Ma" Rainey, the mother of the blues. Her songs give voice to multiple women and their love of good men, love of no-good men, love of themselves, and love of fun times. In defiance of respectability and the Black middle class, she also sang of poverty, prostitution, gambling, partying, and hoodoo. Memphis Minnie's work sees pleasure from multiple perspectives. Her own biography also shows how she pursued her pleasure in music-making, storytelling, and lovemaking.

In Chapter five, I show what it means to be seen by a voyeur. Hughes's blues novel *Not Without Laughter* is heavily influenced by Black women, including his mother. I discuss Hughes's perspective of how respectability divided Black communities and muted Black women's sexuality. Seeing respectability as an outdated lifestyle, he presents a blues woman named Harriet, the daughter of Hager, a former enslaved Christian washerwoman. Readers are introduced to a defiant teenager who uses her talents and her body to escape her hometown in pursuit of a career as a blues singer. Although her life choices alienate her from the women in her family, it is her determination to liberate her body from the restrictions of respectability that make it possible for her to be a major resource to her nephew. Hughes draws attention to Aunt Hager's three daughters, all of whom represent a type that ranges between respectability (Tempy), unrequited desires (Annjee), and resistance to respectable living (Harriet). This chapter also sees the influences of Hughes's mother, Carrie, an amateur actress, in this work. Carrie Hughes's failed pursuit of pleasure through acting resonates in her son's novel.

These women are hardly representative of the masses of Black women all over the country who made personal decisions that went undocumented and were unseen by the world. Yet, the decisions they made during the interwar era to delve into their own unique expressions of creativity in a society that could be hostile toward Black women were valiant attempts to enhance the lives of the women discussed in *See Me Naked*. Ultimately, what we may learn from these women is how they tapped into their creative personas to find inner peace, not necessarily perfect peace, but a peace that gave them a sense of satisfaction that could not be disturbed by external forces. If we listen closely to the women's narratives, we too may find our own center of pleasure.

1

Finding Yolande Du Bois's Pleasure

On April 9, 1928, Yolande Du Bois wed Countee Cullen in a much-talked-about ceremony. As Yolande's famous father W.E.B. Du Bois had expected, the wedding symbolized the pride of the New Negro when it brought together his beloved daughter, who was his only child, and his talented protégée. However, the attention that the couple received after their wedding was not at all what Du Bois was hoping for. Some of the same newspapers that marked the occasion of the large, fancy wedding also marked the couple's divorce the following year. This chapter seeks to bring Yolande Du Bois from underneath the shadow of Du Bois and the public scrutiny of her short-lived marriage.

Yolande Du Bois was born at the dawn of the twentieth century and entered adulthood during the interwar era. She would, as Cheryl Wall in her study of Black women writers of the Harlem Renaissance notes, "bear the burdens of the past most visibly."[1] After the death of their infant son, Burghardt, Nina and William Du Bois welcomed Nina Yolande Du Bois in 1900. Until her untimely death in 1961, Yolande, as she was more often referred to, was always expected to live up to being the daughter of *the* W.E.B. Du Bois. Yet, it goes without saying that any woman has an identity that is not simply attached to or an extension of her parents (regardless of how well known they may be), her spouse, or anyone else she may know. Yolande is no exception. To say the least, as she grew up she had a life of privilege that set her apart from other Black girls her age. Though much can be said about the level of access she had in a segregated America less than fifty years after the abolishment of slavery in 1865, she also was her father's representative for the advocacy of a racial uplift. Du Bois's restrictive prescriptions on Black people and women in particular meant that Yolande was born into an ideal of Black womanhood that Du Bois expressed in his work but did not necessarily practice in his relationship with his wife. This chapter is dedicated to learning more about how Yolande Du Bois negotiated and navigated the ideal of Black womanhood that her father impressed upon his only daughter. Du Bois was a doting and domineering father, making it a challenge for scholars to separate Yolande from the man who had a major influence on her. Although attention to Yolande has been as an extension of studies about her father or her first husband, my focus here is to look specifically at Yolande Du Bois Williams to uncover who she was as a woman—an identity that she would develop beyond her role as daughter. More specifically, for our purposes, I am interested in how and where she found and defined pleasure. Before she became engaged to Cullen, she had begun to take pleasure in her artistic talents and to build a career as an educator. In order to *see* Yolande as an individual before she became the subject of a debacle, I offer a profile of her life that focuses on a period of discovery beginning with her time at Fisk University when she was free to explore the pleasures of love and other forms of enjoyment.

When Yolande went to college in 1920, she went under the influence of Du Bois, who wrote about the problems the race faced, including his position on the role of Black women. How W.E.B. Du Bois felt about women, in general, has been debated among scholars. Clues to how to characterize him may depend largely on the time of his long life and the era. In her article, "Black Feminists and Du Bois: Respectability, Protection, and Beyond," Black feminist scholar Farah Jasmine Griffin takes note of specific work Du Bois published between 1907 and 1920 that championed the cause and position of women, including his poem "Burden of Black Womanhood" and essays "Black Mother," "Hail

Columbia," and "The Damnation of Women." Griffin argues, "More than any other African American thinker of his time or before, Du Bois devoted a great deal of his attention to the condition of black women specifically and distinct from black men."[2] She goes on to note that "Black feminist intellectuals acknowledge Du Bois's sexism in his personal life (specifically his treatment of his daughter), but many of them also applaud his efforts on behalf of black women and claim him as an intellectual ancestor."[3] These scholars include Beverly Guy-Sheftall, Claudia Tate, Joy James, and Hazel Carby. Joining these scholars, Garth E. Pauley argues, "Du Bois's commitment to woman suffrage stemmed from his womanist outlook and his critique of social and political hierarchies, including patriarchal ones."[4] Du Bois's biographer, David Levering Lewis, sees him as a "public feminist." Assessing some of his work, such as "The Burden of Black Women" (1907) and "The Damnation of Women" (1921), and especially his novel *The Quest of the Silver Fleece: A Novel* (1911), Lewis concluded, "*The Quest* reflected the force and sincerity of Du Bois's feminism, his credo that the degree of society's enlightenment and of the empowerment of disadvantaged classes and races was ultimately to be measured by its willingness to emancipate women—and, above all, black women."[5] Seeing reflections of Du Bois's ideas about womanhood imposed on his daughter, Lewis draws a connection by arguing that Du Bois was set apart from other late-Victorian husbands and fathers who "were determined to shelter their womenfolk from overexposure to education and public life. Du Bois's marching orders commanded Yolande to become superlatively educated and emancipated."[6] He wanted to see her as "wise," "moral," and "cosmopolitan."[7] Indeed, his letters to his daughter and his business records related to her living expenses show that Yolande was most certainly sheltered. Living under the patriarchal supervision of a man who touted the importance of Black folks presenting respectable selves, at least publicly, narrowed her potential of enjoying pleasure, as her life choices were severely limited by a father who, as Tonya Bolden notes, "was more obsessed with their daughter's mind." She goes on, "He wanted her to be a little him, a little busy-brained genius. That wasn't Yolande."[8] Du Bois's practice of "feminism," if it was that, did not necessarily extend to his daughter. She was, after all, his daughter and not an ideal of a woman or a movement. Although, how he treated her and what he wanted for and from her was almost always in relation to Black folks. Ultimately, what is lost in Lewis's estimation is Yolande's possibility of developing an identity that did not meet the idyllic expectations of her father.

Yolande's parents were married until Nina's death in 1950. Lewis characterizes Nina Du Bois as a woman who was "an effaced and dutiful wife," "possessed average intelligence," and "was caring, though perhaps not warm . . . and loyal and resourceful."[9] As is obvious from their long separations and businesslike letters to one another, there was a lack of "intimacy" and unspoken "estrangement."[10] By the time Yolande was born, "the marriage had begun to fray years ago. Burghardt's death left a rift. Yolande's birth didn't bridge the gap, but it left Nina obsessive about keeping home and daughter germ-free."[11] Marriage, for the two, was an arrangement that Du Bois believed in as a way to advance the race. It was the way to "negate white stereotypes about the black family," a concept especially important to Du Bois who had been reared in a home without his father.[12] For Du Bois, who had many affairs during their marriage, maintaining the public façade of marriage to people outside his elite circle was more important than how the married couple felt about one another. Nina was provided for and doors were open to her based on her marriage to her husband; therefore, she had a role in society as Mrs. Du Bois and as her namesake's mother. The latter, in particular, was uniquely hers. In letters, Du Bois at times appeared protective of his wife and at least cared about providing for her materially. There appeared to be little by way of emotional support, however. Surely, their daughter was aware of the lack of pleasure her parents took from their marriage.

This chapter relies heavily on letters written to and from Yolande to uncover her too-often silenced voice. In their study of women writers' letters, Jennifer Cognard-Black and Elizabeth MacLeod Walls find, "Letters have served both as a perfunctory form of communication and as a treasured mechanism for articulating women's artistry."[13] In Yolande Du Bois's letters we find a self that emerged, depending on the recipient. With her father, she made requests and probed him for his approval on certain subjects. When communicating with her mother, she was more open about the good times she was having or the pains she was suffering or had suffered. In conversation with Countee Cullen, she was a carefree but mature artist who was not ashamed of her feelings and emotions.

Throughout her life, Yolande's relationship with her father depended largely on the frequency of letters that were exchanged. Before he moved from their home in New York, he traveled as a researcher, organizer, and speaker. As early as 1907, when she was seven years old, Du Bois wrote to his daughter. After asking her about how she liked to play and telling her about the joy he received from sliding when he was a child, he ended by letting her know that he missed his little girl.[14] Du Bois's letters and actions revealed him to be a man who often showed softness and love for his daughter. She may very well have been his greatest vulnerability. Their relationship was built on separation, as Yolande and her mother did not live with Du Bois for most of Yolande's childhood.

From these exchanges, Yolande would learn about writing. Cognard-Black and Walls observe, "Until very recently, moreover, letters symbolized high cultural status and value: literacy, resources, and authority. Letters were often (though not always) preserved and venerated."[15] Du Bois's letters were models for his daughter in this regard as they were samples of his own ability to provide a narrative portrait. At the age of seven, she read his detailed description of the scenery and weather.[16] From him she may have learned how to be attentive of her surroundings, an apt lesson for a girl who often expressed her feelings in relation to others and to events. Though it is not unusual for children to be encouraged to embrace their creative sides, her primary exposure to her father as a writer probably made her feel that she could present this aspect of herself to him. Some of the pieces that he kept of hers include a short story about a goose and a monkey (1908) and a Christmas card

(1910). It is no wonder why she would eventually become an English teacher with an interest in art and drama. If the drawing on the card was done by Yolande, and it probably was, it shows her aptitude for art just as much as the story shows her developing ability to tell a story. What we find is her potential as an artist, a creative form of pleasure she would develop into a career.

Thirteen years later, at the advanced age of twenty, Yolande entered her father's alma mater, Fisk, in fall 1920. Du Bois would remain central in the work she did there. As long as he was her sole financial provider, he could certainly justify exerting some level of control over her. He was also, as Griffin terms it, the one who gave her a "promise of protection."[17] Griffin explains, "Because black women were denied the privileges of femininity and protection from physical and discursive violence, black intellectuals and activists developed a discourse of protection."[18] For Du Bois, he would lead in public discourse, but when it came to his daughter, the promise of protection was how he saw his role as father. The problem, of course, was that his consistent provisions meant that she would learn little about how to manage her own financial affairs and would struggle with independence until her death.

Nevertheless, Fisk was an environment where she thrived and began to flirt with pleasure. After dealing with racial discrimination at the racially mixed Brooklyn Girls' High School,[19] she was now living in the South for the first time in her adult life and was surrounded exclusively by Black folks. It was, indeed, a new experience of which she took to rather easily. Entering Fisk gave her an opportunity to explore her interests and develop her talents. With her father's assistance, she was admitted into the esteemed Jubilee Hall that was designated for Jubilee Singers. A historic musical group, the choir had begun touring as early as 1877, ten years after Fisk University had been incorporated. According to university records, she was not a Jubilee Singer but may have been a member of the glee club. What is clear from her letters is that Yolande enjoyed being a part of the choir. Of her experience regarding what must have been her first jubilee concert, she wrote to her mother of how excited and pleased she was with the event and enclosed a photo to capture her pleasure. As pictured on the cover, the photo shows a young, smiling Yolande who wore the requisite white dress and held a doll[20]

Looking good and enjoying social activities were of the utmost importance to the daughter of Dr. Du Bois, who had commissioned a dressmaker for her. Letters she wrote to her mother often gave details about her wardrobe and the related expenses. Apparently, she kept a busy social schedule. In addition to everyday clothing, she had appropriate dresses to wear to the many socials she attended. Her mother encouraged it by sending catalogs. In the same letter that she described oral surgery she noted that she recovered from the pain of the tooth and went to a social event. Coming from an elite upper-middle-class family, such socializing was not only expected but was part of the lifestyle she had become accustomed to living.[21]

Their lifestyle also saw the arts as important. Records show that Du Bois consistently paid extra fees in support of Yolande's music education while at Fisk. In addition to singing, she also danced. She described being in the front row of a dance on Spring Day. She shared a compliment she received from an elder woman about her dancing abilities. Delving into artistic expression was an enjoyable experience for Yolande, who loved the arts and the creative energy that emerged from exploring various mediums of expression from drawing and dancing to singing and playing music. Her father indulged her at first by sending her money to purchase a banjo ukulele, which she said she learned to play two songs on. Du Bois probably knew that she was not very good at playing instruments and may not have been very good at dancing or singing either, but these were activities that brought her so much joy that any small step of accomplishment she made she shared with her father in hopes of winning his approval. Eventually Du Bois tired of his daughter's musical interests and, in her third year, he advised her not to take music, as he saw it as extra work that she was not able to easily handle.

Yet, Yolande would find other ways to express herself. She wrote to her parents mostly of her accomplishments, namely those things that brought her pleasure, such as performing or dressing for a social event. To her mother, she spoke of her physical appearance, to her father she told of compliments she had received for having done something. It was him that she told of her excitement of making the dean's list and warned him that the good grades she got that quarter may not occur again.[22] College was a place where she experienced typical highs and lows.

During the summer before her sophomore year, she decided that she would declare a major in English. This likely accounts for the creative writing she sent to her father. Yolande's interest in writing received a national audience when she wrote a sketch for a 1920 *The Brownies'* Book issue. *The Brownies'* focused on Africa and the diaspora by printing positive images of Black children from around the world alongside stories that were told about Africa. One of the magazine's purposes was to give Black children a positive image of themselves that counteracted the more common pictures in the media of pickaninnies. The essay attributed to her, titled "A Curious Geography Lesson," attempts to inform readers about Menelik, the emperor of Abyssinia, and his quest for independence from European rule. The story is told to two young siblings by their mother. Du Bois's influence is apparent in this story. He is known to have written many such articles on the state of colonial Africa and its history for *The Crisis*, the NAACP's journal. He wrote for *The Brownies'* as well. The story is a bit sophisticated for a young audience, as it gives dates and suggests that the children read *The Brownies'*, newspapers, and *The Literary Digest* so that they can enhance their knowledge of geography and history. It has very little description or imagination and limited dialogue. Instead, it relies on telling the history. In many ways, the short story, which is more of a historical profile, points to the limited resources there were for Black readers of any age to learn more about Africa. Despite being heavily influenced by Du Bois, it presupposes the kind of knowledge of history and geography that Yolande would certainly bring to the classroom at the segregated schools where she taught in later years.

By contrast, a short story published under her name in the last issue of *The Brownies'* (December 1921) is a record of Yolande's creative voice. In "The Land Behind the Sun" twenty-one-year-old Yolande presented a fairy tale about a little brown girl who is put to bed by her mother for performing a number of naughty acts. Before she leaves her daughter, the mother teases her imagination by threatening that the "Brownies will come and carry you away." Indeed, something does come to take her away, a mythical small figure. Delving into her imagination, Yolande says the little girl named Madeline sees a curious small person made of gold. The Brownie, as she comes to learn, is not meant to scare Madeline, who is only astonished by its presence; in fact, she is intrigued and willing to travel with the winged figure to the land behind the sun. In this new world, she learns that the Wicked Witch of Bogland captures naughty children, and she has the opportunity to destroy the witch and rescue the captured king.

Yolande writes an empowering story where a little brown girl becomes a hero. Rather than the king or prince saving the captured girl, the girl emerges as an intuitive protector. Further, the Brownies are powerful girls. They are small and unseen, but they protect brown children. The voice of African American women and girls is prominent in both the short story and the earlier historical profile disguised as a short story. In both, mothers are influential in how their children think about the world outside their own. They are encouraged to learn, to travel to foreign lands, and to imagine themselves outside of the United States. Travel resonates loudly in the two works and travel suggests freedom from oppression of the mind and the physical state. Through Yolande's voice and in keeping with *The Brownies'* magazine, Yolande used her imagination and her own experience with domestic and international travel to transform and inspire young minds. Du Bois gave her a place to publish, and probably some guidance, as he believed that she had talent he wanted to cultivate and encourage for the good of the race. Unfortunately, how Yolande felt about this aspect of her work is not known.

Nevertheless, *The Crisis* was where she received national exposure for her developing art skills. On the cover of the April 1922 edition, there is a winged flapper girl holding a flowing ribbon. Her legs are in the stance of a dance move. In the left corner of the cover is a little girl. Perhaps the girl is dreaming of the freedom and defiance that is represented by the flapper girl. Of the "brazen flappers," Carol Dyhouse says, "they horrified conservatives by blowing cigarette smoke in the face of Victorian ideas of feminine constraint and decorum."[23] At the dawn of the jazz age, a twenty-two-year-old college sophomore depicted her generation. Through the image a feeling of freedom and defiance is conveyed to the audience of *The Crisis*. Curiously, the girl looks White as so many images of the flapper girl tended to be. Yet, Yolande was at Fisk and was most certainly exposed to jazz while there and probably more so when she went home during the summers.

Known for her pleasant attitude, it was also at Fisk that she fell in love. It was there that she pursued her interest in several young men, including Cullen. According to Cullen's biographer Charles Molesworth, their relationship began as a friendship as early as summer 1923 when the two were introduced by Cullen's companion Harold Jackman and developed as the two bonded over their artistic interests. She began to write to him after her father rebuffed her interest in Jimmie Lunceford in May. On December 3, 1923, she wrote what was likely her first letter to Cullen where she explains to him that she was motivated to write after reading in the newspaper that he had won an award. She goes on to express her pride in his accomplishment. Yolande's flirtatious and confident persona emerged in what became a series of letters to Cullen. Obviously, Cullen liked the surprise of the letter and showed his interest in her by writing back. Without his letters, her responses to him not only show the pleasure she took in how corresponding with him made her feel happy but also the pleasure he took in their developing relationship. Enamored by his ability to share his lyrical talents with her in the form of a letter, Yolande freely, although cautiously, wrote of her growing affection for the poet.[24] Leaning in to his words (his letters are not available) and her emotions, Yolande engaged in a period of discovery and exploration of feelings where love is possible.

As their letter writing continued, she complimented him on more than his poetic talents, including his eyes, hands, and intellect. Cullen kept these letters, as they are now a part of his archive at the Beinecke Library, suggesting how much he appreciated the bond they developed and the emotions she expressed. Perhaps it was simply an appeal to his ego or he felt genuine affection for her.

A turn in their relationship is marked by a letter she wrote to him after a visit to Baltimore where she made a confession. It may be that she told Cullen of her attraction to Jimmie Lunceford, a love interest she developed during her matriculation at Fisk. After Cullen left, she wrote that she felt badly about whatever she had shared with him.[25] What actually occurred was not reiterated in the letters, but she took the blame for the unwritten offense. As a result, she asked him to deal gently with her feelings for him.

There was confusion when it came to her dreams. Lunceford was not a priority, according to Du Bois in a letter to Yolande in 1923 where he mentions both Lunceford and another man that she apparently had been dating. Du Bois seemed weary from his daughter who seemed to be focusing too much on relationships with men and not enough on her studies and he was not impressed with this new man. Of course, he may have known about Cullen and was holding out hope for a permanent union. Lunceford's enrollment at Fisk was not enough to impress Du Bois. Born in Fulton, Mississippi, in 1902, James Melvin "Piggie" Lunceford graduated from Fisk with a bachelor's in sociology in 1925. She probably met him through her musical studies at Fisk. Surely, he impressed Yolande with his musical and sports skills. In addition to playing in the orchestra and singing in the glee club, he played football and baseball and ran track. Like Yolande, he took a teaching position following graduation. However, teaching music at Manassas High School was not his passion. Lunceford was a performer with dreams of being a renowned big band leader. Three years after starting his career, he began to travel with a band he had assembled.

Yolande and Jimmie had a connection that may have faded over time but continued long after her marriage ended with Cullen. Lewis provides, "Lunceford was Yolande's enduring passion, the man about whom she would spend much of her life dreaming, wondering how different things could have been if they had married."[26] Unfortunately, Lewis does not give any further information about why he arrived at this conclusion. Indeed, Lunceford was only a dream, perhaps the object of passion for which she did not pursue merely because romance does not save the race. Yolande's daughter, Yolande, by her second husband, reported that her mother introduced her to Lunceford at a concert and that the man looked at the two and said, "She should have been mine."[27] In 1930 Jimmie's band recorded two songs, "In Dat Mawnin" and "Sweet Rhythm." The band eventually became a regular performer at the Cotton Club where he worked with up-and-comers such as Lena Horne. Disrupted by World War II drafts and economic instability, Lunceford had minimal commercial success as a jazz band leader. He died from a heart attack on July 13, 1947.

Hopeful, lovestruck Yolande must have told her father that she had a serious love interest, as he wrote to her with hopes of making her rethink any idea of marriage. Du Bois's letter reflected his usual way of presenting the matter as he saw it: love in marriage was nothing without friendship. Yet, although he gave his daughter a rather strong opinion on marriage, he concluded, it was her choice.[28] His advice about marriage is probably about Jimmie. Du Bois would have been more encouraging had she been referring to Cullen. Just two years before, on December 31, 1924, Du Bois had written to his daughter about how pleased he was that he and Nina had been surprised with a twenty-fifth wedding anniversary party hosted by Jessie Fauset. Fauset, whom he worked with through the editing of *The Crisis* and *The Brownies'*, and with whom Du Bois had an affair, had hosted the party in her home. Du Bois and Yolande's mother had not lived together for any prolonged period during the time that Yolande was growing up. She most certainly would not have been able to look to them for a model of a marriage between two people who were in love and who were friends. Unable to enjoy the experience of close paternal bonds, Yolande was most likely looking for both love and companionship.

Besides juggling love affairs, schoolwork, and a busy social life, Yolande was in poor health and had been since her childhood. During her third year at Fisk, in fall 1922, she suffered from appendicitis and problems with her ovaries. As a result, she had to have an appendectomy and cysts removed from her ovaries. Without the physical support of her parents, she went into recovery and began to make progress until she had a setback in May 1923. Then she reportedly suffered from a postsurgical illness. By August, she received a letter from her father about the nuances of marriage. It is likely, then, that in her parents' absence, she developed a bond with the man she was considering to be her husband, Jimmie Lunceford.

Though her illness had an impact on her studies, she persisted and managed to graduate from Fisk. Despite Yolande saying in an earlier letter to her father that she had no interest in teaching, she found herself walking in her father's footsteps, first as a student at Fisk and then moving into the teaching profession. It was certainly not unusual for women of her era to pursue such careers. Black women in "professional service" were most likely to either teach or to become nurses. In this way, they would fulfill their duties of advancing the race by serving those who were in need. In anticipation of Yolande finishing her requirements at some point between 1925 and 1926, Du Bois wrote to her and asked her to begin an earnest search for a teaching position. So committed was he to her being successful that he actually sent her a draft of a letter and a list of schools to send it to. She received an offer for a teaching position and Du Bois, using his vast experience, advised her not to accept any offer until she learned more about the salary; this would also give her time to see if any other offers came in. With this level of nuanced oversight and mentorship, when was she ever to learn how to become an independent woman?[29]

Yolande was on the brink of embarking on a career and presumably would have been moving into a new phase of independence for the first time in her life. He had been paying her bills throughout her schooling and advising her on how to manage the money he sent her. In some ways, she lived a privileged lifestyle, as she enjoyed access to information that many of her Black peers did not have. From his perspective, she was not good at managing money. This is not a surprising revelation. At one point, he strongly admonished her for using a pawnshop.[30] To avoid making such decisions, he also told her that she needed to learn to get on with very little.[31] Given the constraints that she endured with her mother while attending school in England during World War I, she certainly knew what it was like to live a financially lean life. However, he always provided for his only child.

Upon graduation, she committed herself to developing her academic knowledge and artistic talents. Du Bois gave his daughter a rare compliment in 1923 when at Fisk he told her that "you have the ability to write and draw—but these talents need long and painstaking cultivation." He went on to tell her that such cultivation could enhance the "success" of a happy marriage. In a move toward "cultivating" her talents, Yolande enrolled in Columbia University where she studied English with a specialty in teaching English and drawing. According to her, she took four classes in English and three in drawing, a rather heavy load for a woman who was also teaching full-time. This would be the first time in her academic life when she would embrace academic rigor. Du Bois was proud of his daughter's accomplishments, which included more than just her scholarly and career pursuits.

Embracing her career would not keep her from finding a suitable match, as she knew her father wanted her to marry. In a letter Du Bois wrote to Francis Hoggan,[32] he referenced her engagement to Mr. Phelton (*sic*) Clark, who had received a bachelor's degree from Beloit and, like Yolande, a master's from Columbia in 1925. They must have met during their graduate studies in New York. Du Bois characterized Clark as a promising young man. The son of the founder of Southern University in Baton Rouge prompted

Du Bois's glowing remarks. Surely, he saw his daughter's choice in a fiancé as suitable. He wrote, Clark is "well-bred" smart man of "excellent character." At some point the union ended, however. Curiously, there is no formal announcement of this engagement in the newspapers, indicating that it must have ended almost as soon as it began. Whatever occurred, it shows her willingness to be in a relationship, to give in to the vulnerability of coupling. What Cullen knew of this engagement is not known, but it did not stop her from writing to him regularly.

Beyond her rather complicated love life, she embraced her teaching career at the Senior High School for Colored (later the Frederick Douglass High School) in Baltimore, Maryland, one of two high schools for Black children in the city. As Cullen was enrolled at New York University, she continued to write to him about her burgeoning career and, of course, growing feelings for him. On May 10, 1926, she wrote, "the redeeming feature of teaching is the friendship." Later that night she wrote to him about the inconveniences of a fire that destroyed part of her classroom and that her heart was broken by the fact that the workmen's presence kept her from holding any classes. Yolande most certainly enjoyed teaching, as her expression of annoyance for having her time in the classroom disrupted shows. She took pride in her work and love of her children, "Our 'Revue' was a grand success. I was so proud of my children."[33] Other than her feelings about Cullen, Yolande remained positive despite the stress of her job. The delight she took in teaching children seemed to distract her from preparing for the teacher's exam. In the same letter she shared her delight with Cullen, that the children had brought her spring flowers. [34] Such a small but thoughtful gesture was motivation for the work she had to do to continue teaching the children she had come to adore.

During this period, she led a full and busy life. In addition to her first full-time job as a teacher, she continued to find pleasure in her relationship with Cullen. In support of his studies, she wrote to him that her love for him did not depend on him having degrees.[35] As was consistent with her letter writing of this period, she talked about her work and then expressed her deep affection for him.[36] Her feelings for Cullen developed and she was disappointed when he did not respond promptly to her letters. A lack of a letter meant, among other things, that whatever she was feeling she was unable to share it with a willing participant. Writing to Cullen gave her an opportunity to convey a level of sensuality that was part of their relationship. Her longings for him grew rather intense as seen in her letter of June 6, 1926, where she confessed her desire for him, presumably physical. How he felt about her sexual overtures the archive does not reveal, but the fact that she felt a freedom with him that became more pronounced over the years suggests that he did not discourage these confessions. June proved to be an active time for their relationship to develop further as she wrote freely in response to his inquiries about her happiness with him. In fact, it appears he had or was contemplating telling his mother about their relationship, to which she expressed concern of not being accepted. Keeping their written relationship between the two, she only mentioned her father once and that was about a visit he made to Baltimore.

Yolande's career and her relationship with Cullen, by her own admission, brought her immense pleasure. With Cullen's encouragement, her letters to him were a creative outlet through which she could express her emotions and desires. She may have revealed a self to him that was unknown by anyone else. Cullen took a trip to Paris in August 1926, and they continued to write to one another. In response to at least one letter she received from him, again she shared her longing that left her feeling sad. And, later, while at school, she told him that she thought of him as she played the Victrola for the children, which made her remember dancing with him.[37] This is the first time that she makes a reference to them going out together and having fun. Her letter also references not only the free movement of dancing but a sharing of an experience that undoubtedly brought them together as one touched the other. By then, she began to sign off with an expression of love. Yolande was clearly in love with the poet and she was willing to confess her feelings unashamedly.

During the month of September, she became more comfortable expressing her wantonness. More specifically, on September 12, 1926, she told him she wished he could "see her room." There is a sexual implication here as much as there is a factor of respectability that made such visits, and invitations for them, improper. Therefore, she made a trip to see him the following weekend. It was a lovely trip that left her feeling the desire to convey how being with him brought her joy and a wonderful sense of satisfaction.

Being near him would come soon. Along with her close friend Margaret Wellmon, Yolande sailed to England in June 1927. She spent much of the summer and early fall in Paris where she studied French. Upon their return in September, invitations were sent to several people to dine with Yolande and Miss Wellmon; among the invitees was Countee Cullen. Given the fact that Yolande had spent several months in France, they certainly had much to discuss, as Cullen was quite found of Paris. Who sent the invitation or why it was initiated is unknown, but after at least three years of correspondence, they must have been ready to court formally. The two became engaged, much to the delight of Du Bois and the Black elite in 1927. One paper's notice sensationalized the announcement, "Although the couple had been engaged for some time, the engagement was kept a secret until now. When Mr. Cullen purchased an apartment in the new Paul Laurence Dunbar Garden Apartments . . . the engagement became rumored, but inquiries met with a denial."[38] Both Cullen and Yolande were under constant public scrutiny, and the public awaited a grand affair. The article goes on, "The wedding is expected to be one of the most brilliant social affairs of the early spring season." Du Bois took the lead to make it so.

What we learn from the extensive number of letters that Du Bois exchanged with his daughter is that he was centrally involved as the coordinator of the wedding. We also hear his voice in terms of intervening with the relationship itself. Du Bois hardly recognized any boundaries when it came to his daughter's life, especially her intimate affairs. Here, he did not hold back and he fully expected his daughter to listen to his direction.

Yolande's communications with her fiancé were not guaranteed to be kept between the two. Du Bois greatly admired Cullen, and the two had their own relationship, as Du Bois frequently featured his poetry in *The Crisis*. It is not clear who wanted to please Du Bois more, Yolande or Cullen, but a gender bias that favors Cullen emerges in this father-daughter-son-in-law relationship, and Cullen took advantage of it. Yolande was living in Baltimore and was at a disadvantage. While she corresponded with her father by letter, Cullen and Du Bois had lunch together in New York and made decisions. It was also during those lunches that Cullen confided in the patriarch. He understood that a close bond with Du Bois was a boost to his career, including a letter that Du Bois had written for him to receive the Guggenheim. Marrying Yolande bonded him even closer to Du Bois. The patriarch made no secret of the fact that his relationship with Cullen meant that he was privy to what they discussed and would intervene. This became abundantly clear when he brazenly discouraged her from pressing Cullen to pursue a doctorate or a teaching career.[39] As the editor of *The Crisis*, his concern was that she would hinder Cullen's ability to create. He would go on to explain that a doctorate was not necessary for Cullen's generation although it was for his. Du Bois, the race activist, seemed to be suggesting progress and stability that Black people had achieved in the sixty years since slavery had been enough. Dyhouse observes, "Social stability was seen to depend on a right ordering of male and female, and on the protection of daughters. . . . Protection was a two-edged sword, and it frequently shaded into control."[40] What is obvious here was that what he was willing to concede for Cullen, he was not for his daughter. Du Bois wanted his daughter to receive a formal education, and although he did not press her to pursue a doctorate, he constantly encouraged her to pursue additional studies. Cullen's talent, if not his personality, had won over the patriarch.

As expressed in earlier correspondence, Du Bois was adamant that his daughter make wedding arrangements based on a budget, for he was a man of limited means. As the only child of a well-respected man, Yolande never seemed fully aware that her father was not wealthy. Yet, she resisted what she may have perceived as him trying to put limits on her happiness. This was a rare opportunity for her to shine on a national stage, unlike her father and fiancé who were consistently being seen and praised for their work. To be sure, she liked the spotlight as she described in her letters to her mother about her activities at Fisk. Yolande was determined to be "cute" on her wedding day set for April 9, 1928. In their exchanges, conversation about financial matters was a power tug-of-war, a matter of who was in charge. Yolande was the bride who was to be a public spectacle and would, as the daughter of the famous intellectual, marry a man her father greatly admired. In a rather pointed letter he told her to reduce the number of her bridesmaids from fifteen to four or five. To plan for 200 guests. And, to honeymoon in the Northeast.[41] Du Bois's entreaties were futile. He would continue to tell her to cut the number of bridesmaids, but as time went on, he began to relent on the number by asking her to cut from fifteen to six. Perhaps Du Bois was willing to compromise, but certainly his daughter's unwillingness to acquiesce informed him that he was not always in control. As Jeffrey O. G. Ogbar concludes, "Despite the expense of the wedding and reception, Du Bois eventually saw the pomp and circumstance as an emblem of the progress of African Americans."[42] The African American press posted announcements and postnuptial news, usually leading with a title that favored Cullen, such as "Countee Cullen to Marry Daughter of Dr. W.E.B. Du Bois." Ultimately, as *The New York Age* described, in addition to Wellmon, her maid of honor, Yolande had sixteen bridesmaids.[43] Cullen's best man was Harold Jackman. Langston Hughes was an usher. Du Bois covered the grandest of affairs, complete with photographs, in the June 1928 *The Crisis*.

After they honeymooned in the Northwest, Cullen, along with his father and Harold Jackman, set sail for Paris, where Cullen was to write his poetry with the support of the prestigious Guggenheim Fellowship. In the scantily written journal he kept of the time, Cullen hardly mentioned his wife,[44] who joined them later. Du Bois wrote to his daughter with his expectations. He impressed upon his daughter his ideal of who she should be by emphasizing the importance of working—to become an anatomy artist, to become fluent in French, and most of all, to be a helpmate to her husband. Du Bois seemed always to think of his daughter in relation to solving the problems of the race. Her voice was his voice. Their voice was what the race needed to succeed. Yolande's plans may not have been considered, but they were not aligned with her father's.

Meanwhile, Yolande was silent in her correspondence with her father and mother. The patriarch did not appear to consider what Yolande may have wanted from her time in Paris or from her new marriage. If he bothered to ask, it's not in the archive. She certainly was interested in art, but the aspects of her interests were not asked or encouraged. She was merely told what her interests should be. In other words, she was to consider work that would be attractive to an audience, that would have some purpose other than her own. Taking pleasure in her own individual interests was not an option that her father would allow, as these were merely to make her the center of attention. Her job was to be a supportive wife to Cullen rather than a distraction by helping him to stay focused on his writing. Du Bois advised her to do this by not thinking of herself, but of her husband. As his daughter and as made clear in his letter, there was no room in his vision for Yolande to have the luxury of "herself." Two things are conveyed in his message to his daughter. One, Du Bois saw his daughter as a possible disruption to the kind of Black genius that he felt Cullen embodied. Two, Du Bois had no tolerance for women to enjoy pleasure unless it was of a variety that involved work and self-sacrifice. Du Bois wanted his daughter to be to Cullen what Nina was to him.

While Du Bois instructed his daughter to "make it easy for Countee to write," he had expectations for Cullen as well. Du Bois wrote to Cullen to ask him to send reflections on his time in Europe and asked that Yolande illustrate those articles. What he could not have known was that his daughter was dealing with the reality of her failing marriage. Thinking little of his daughter's ability to perform as a proper wife, he took whatever Cullen told him about

Yolande as truth. As usual, Du Bois was involved with the couple's affairs; whatever judgments he had of them he did not hesitate to keep to himself, especially when it came to his opinion of his daughter. Cullen's correspondence with his father-in-law had the effect, as he knew it would, of extinguishing the voice of his wife. Whatever he told Du Bois about Yolande, Du Bois reacted with harsh criticism of his daughter, whom he felt was being unreasonable, but he was in support of the marriage because he was convinced that she loved Cullen.[45] Relying on Cullen's word and not consulting with his daughter led him to conclude that her distance from Cullen was due to sexual inexperience.[46] He asked his son-in-law to be patient, but not to send her back to the United States before Christmas. Feminist scholar bell hooks reminds us, "For men, satisfying sexual desire became more important than the art of loving. Sex could take precedence over life because it was like work, a domain where one could engage in power plays."[47] Cullen's attempt to divert the gaze from him by casting the blame on his wife was encouraged by Du Bois, who assumed that his daughter was the cause of their troubles. The truth was that a reconciliation was not possible. On May 23, 1929, less than a year after their spectacular wedding, she and Cullen were ready to file for divorce.

Du Bois, who as scholars such as his biographer Lewis have documented led a very active sex life through multiple extramarital affairs, pled his daughter's case with her husband. Du Bois's presumptions were based on the male-centered perspective offered by the patriarch who, although a researcher, had little information to draw conclusions about his daughter's situation or experience. Letters of her expression of longing for Cullen before their marriage strongly suggest that she had sexual desire for him and she was certain that she felt as though she loved him, sentiments that he encouraged and embraced. But for Yolande, her desire was private and was to be shared with the man she loved. Acknowledging Cullen's disappointment for the lack of sexual pleasure he said he was receiving from his wife, Du Bois asked his son-in-law to build a marriage based on love as he had. Pledging his love as his second father, Du Bois expressed his support and encouragement for the surrogate son.[48]

In this exchange, Yolande's voice was silenced. Her desires that she so liberally shared with Cullen in her letters a year or so before were taken as absolute. Du Bois incorrectly surmised that his daughter was not just simply unreasonable but that she was unwilling to be the woman that men decided a woman should be. Jennifer Nash observes, "I do not imagine pleasure as existing outside of inequality, violence, or pain, nor do I imagine pleasure to circulate outside the systems of domination which constrain us."[49] Yolande was overshadowed by this historical narrative and the "system of domination" as a woman stuck in a triangle that consisted of a husband who had no desire for her and a father who assumed that she was responsible for sexually satisfying her husband. It was not possible to meet the desires of either her father or her husband when it came to her body.

Months later, Yolande's voice would be heard on the reason for the lack of sexual intimacy among the two.[50] After her marriage ended, she wrote to her father that she heard from other people who told her of Cullen's attraction for men. The dismayed young bride expressed a feeling of shock upon learning that her husband enjoyed the sexual company of men, a lifestyle that she knew very little about and had not considered. Yolande's reaction to this was mixed. She seemed to have gone through stages of processing the reality of the situation she faced. At first, she was mad and felt betrayed, and then, she pitied him. Perhaps the latter was a remnant of the love that she would say she never felt for the man. Earlier letters to him certainly suggest otherwise, but her feelings of anger made her forget those earlier days of how he made her feel. Being sheltered in the interwar era, for Yolande, meant living among people who did not speak of, let alone openly engage in, same-sex relationships. Any such relationships were discussed as petty gossip. Writing to her father out of necessity, she seemed to be apologetic for having married Cullen. For Yolande, this was deeply personal, as she asked her father to burn the letter and confided in him that she had not told her mother and did not want to make it grounds for divorce. Why did Du Bois keep a copy of the letter, revealing the real reason for the demise of his only daughter's first marriage? Perhaps feeling that she had failed her father, she wrote at least twice that if she had known previous to taking her vows she would not have married him.

Her letter seemed to have made a difference to her father who was in the position of representing the family on this matter. After Du Bois issued a statement about the divorce, Charles Edgerton wrote to Du Bois to express his condolences. Du Bois responded that neither party was to blame for the dissolution of marriage. Du Bois's response is both protective of his daughter and sympathetic toward his former son-in-law. Nevertheless, Yolande bet on love and she felt betrayed. Ironically, the demise of her marriage freed her from living under Cullen's shadow. Without him, people would have to deal with her as Yolande, at times as the daughter of Du Bois, but most certainly not as the wife of the famous poet. She returned to the United States to her career in teaching as a divorced woman.

Walking away from her marriage, one sanctioned and most certainly highly encouraged by her father, was not an easy action to take. At a time when Du Bois was pushing marriage among educated Blacks to strengthen the race and to raise a generation of educated Black people whose success would stand against the stereotypes presupposed by racism, the promises of his daughter's public marriage was no longer to be. It was, undoubtedly, a frightening step for her to take as much as it was bold. More importantly, it was freeing. After following her father's lead, she could now go forth and make decisions about her future without the same pressure from her father and without trying to conform to a marriage with a man who could not fulfill her physical pleasures.

From Cullen's perspective, he did her a favor in terms of filing for divorce. In making his case to Du Bois for a reimbursement of funds, he told his former father-in-law, "When Mrs. Du Bois was here and learned that I had started proceedings for a divorce on my account, she suggested that I let it be changed on Yolande's account, that I pay the bill and that you would subsequently reimburse me." On this rare occasion, it is revealed that Nina Du Bois acted on behalf of her daughter to protect her reputation. Nina insisted that her daughter not appear to have been abandoned, giving her a sense of empowerment that the well-known Cullen could have taken by filing for divorce. Nevertheless, rumors in the African American newspapers would distort the unspeakable truth in favor of Cullen: "Cullen Suing for Divorce"[51] read one title, in which the writer informed curious readers, "Countee, the report continues 'has a girl somewhere in America whom he really loves and the marriage seems to have been one of convenance [sic] as the French say.'"

There is still a lack of truth, a silencing that exists in his correspondence. Cullen seemed gracious in saying that he would not issue an announcement as "such an announcement should come from her." In none of his correspondence does he tell his part in what led to the divorce. It would seem from Du Bois's responses that she was to blame. Yolande refused to be married in name only. She insisted on more.

After the failure of a relationship with her beloved Jimmie, a short engagement, and a marriage, she would try marriage again. She met Arnette Franklin Williams, a muscular football player who was not a lover of poetry. Indeed, this man, who was attending the city's teacher's college while Yolande was teaching art at the Baltimore school that housed the night school, was the opposite of Cullen. Surely Yolande was trying something new by choosing a man that could satisfy her in ways other than the intellectual bilingual artist. They married in a small ceremony on Wednesday, September 2, 1931. Once again, Du Bois became involved when he paid for his new son-in-law's tuition. He would most certainly not have his daughter married to a man who had no degree any longer than necessary. Williams returned to Lincoln University in Pennsylvania to complete his degree. While completing his studies, the couple had one daughter, named Nina Yolande Du Bois Williams, in October 1932. They called her Baby Du Bois. Unfortunately, Yolande found herself in an abusive marriage and had to file for divorce again.

A second divorce and a daughter left her having to deal with a sense of failure. As her parents had held fast to the façade of marriage and her intellectual father hoped to strengthen the race through family ties and education, he could only point to her success in one area. Yolande continued to teach and to rely on her parents for support. Her mother had lived with her off and on to assist with the rearing of the next generation of Du Bois and had been alarmed by the lifestyle her daughter was leading. According to Nina, their daughter had taken a lover who was ten years her junior.[52] The many years of suppressing her sexual desires to meet the respectable restrictions of her mother and father—who most certainly was not suppressing his—had led to this point in her life. She decided to put herself first. As a result, Baby Du Bois was taken from her mother, who was living in New York, to live with her grandmother and Du Bois in Atlanta, where he was teaching at Atlanta University. It was not a place for a toddler, and Du Bois was not prone to being a full-time father or papa. After a year, Nina and her granddaughter returned to New York to be near Yolande where she was raised with the help of her grandmother and financial support of her grandfather. When Yolande died unexpectedly in 1961 from heart problems, she was a grandmother of a boy.

Nina Yolande Du Bois Williams was named for her mother and was known for being the daughter of W.E.B. Du Bois, but this did not make her a replica of either parent. Who she was and what she desired was too often silenced under the high level of expectations that Black society had of her. Yet, when we look, we find a woman who took steps to explore who she was as just Yolande. Perhaps bell hooks captures her life when she states, "That females are born into a patriarchal world, which first invites us to make the journey to love and then places barriers to our way, is one of life's ongoing tragedies."[53] It was not easy being a Black woman in this world, and Yolande may have still been in process at the end of her rather short life, but even to make the attempt to determine what pleasure meant to her placed her beyond the narrow confines of a respectable life.

2

Lena Horne and Respectable Pleasure

Eventually, when "interested" people began to try to give me
different "images" of myself, I came to realize that nobody
(and certainly not yet myself) had any sound image to give a woman
who stood between the two conventional ideas of Negro womanhood:
the "good," quiet, Negro woman who scrubbed and cooked and
was a respectable servant—and the whore.

—Lena Horne, *Lena*

As a light-skinned woman who was reared in a conservative, race-conscious household similar to Yolande Du Bois's, Lena Horne had much to consider when it came to understanding how to define Negro womanhood. Horne learned very early that her skin color called forth a historical narrative that was mired in an unsavory history of exploitation. When she entered Hollywood, she had to contend with the well-known light-skinned tragic mulatta or jezebel stereotype. Moving forward into the interwar era, representations of lighter-skinned, light-enough-to-pass-for-White women as sexual deviants would persist. Representations of Black women with light skin, long hair, and other European features emerged in the pages of literature and later in the evolving film industry. In these representations of women, questions persist: How does a light-skinned Black woman reject the stigma of the lascivious mulatta so that she can define and enjoy pleasure on her own terms?

Further, to what extent does grappling with the stigma of "miscegenation" require lighter-skinned Black women to perform respectability in public? Lena Horne leveraged the benefits she acquired from her skin color and resisted being confined by it.

Through a reading of her 1965 autobiography, *Lena*, and several of her film roles, I will discuss how Lena Horne built a successful career for herself that satisfied Black people's need for respectable icons as she also teased the stereotype of the sexual mulatta. Horne's life and work delves into ways in which pleasure may be taken, wrested away to further define the self as other than a prescribed body satiated in a set of historical narratives that she did not write. First, her decision to be a performer—a career that gave her a place of her own and an ability to rise above her precarious financial circumstances—allowed Horne to rewrite, revise, and expand her life's narrative for an audience that, at times, defined her based simply on her light skin. As noted by Jennifer Nash, "racialized performances can be pleasurable for subjects on all sides of the proverbial color line."[1] Horne's autobiography speaks from her side of the color line. By doing so, she makes it possible for her audience of readers and visual onlookers to see the performance from multiple angles and consider the implications and inferences. Second, we learn how she searched for pleasure in the decisions she made as a woman—married twice, once to a Black man and then to a White man—and as a performer who learned how to revise the script of the mulatta stereotype. She was also known to have affairs with influential men in the film industry. What may have been most important to Horne was defining who she was irrespective of the expectations of Black people and the sexualizing gaze of onlookers.

Born in 1917, by the time of her death in 2010, Lena Horne had garnered the reputation for successfully navigating racism in the entertainment industry to become a respected singer, dancer, and actress. Taught to always present herself as a lady by her activist grandmother, her troubled mother, and an early mentor, her performative life became a narrative that she would later give voice to in her autobiographies. By extension, her biographers speak of how complicated her personal life actually was.

There is much to question when an autobiographer, especially a performer, expresses that she will represent a real self. Performance extends from the stage to the page. Autobiography is presumably written by the self about the self. But the self is untrustworthy, as there is a tension that exists between the self that is presented for an audience and the self that is reluctant to bear his/her/their soul to the audience. Even more, there is a tension between the facts and the teller's interpretation of the facts. Ultimately, the subject tells a story, and a story can include a variety of colorful lies. Lena Horne cowrites her journey toward establishing a free self in her autobiography, *Lena*. In the book, published in 1965, during the civil rights movement, Horne, who had been expected to be an activist-performer or an activist through her performances, decides that it is time to introduce the real Lena to the world. As such, *Lena* is decidedly race-conscious. Horne's performative-presentation of her self causes her to leave out the truth about her parentage. Refusing to cower to attempts to pass as anyone other than African American, she denies the fact that her mother is White and Afro-Portuguese and that her father was Black, White, and Native American. Neither of her grandfathers was African American, yet her paternal grandfather actually passed as Black when he wrote for a Black newspaper and endured job discrimination in New York.[2]

Horne follows the path of a girl to a woman who constantly remade herself to fit into the changing circumstances of her life. After her parents' divorce, she was often either in her paternal grandmother's care or carried away by her mother to live with people whose names she did not know. Their impressions on her are what drive her memory of the travels through the South, and we never know exactly why her mother is not with her. Although Horne says her mother's absences are due to her search for work, the kind of work that kept her away is not revealed to readers. It's not surprising that her most pleasant times are always when she is not with her mother. In particular, she enjoyed the life she had as a child in the home of her paternal uncle and his wife. There she had her own room and access to books, an experience that contrasted greatly with the time she was physically and verbally abused by a woman with whom her mother left her. When her mother learned of the abuse from a neighbor, she responded by removing young Lena from the woman's house. Her mother asked her why she did not tell her about the abuse; Lena felt as though it was her duty to protect her mother. There is a sense in her response that she feels a level of responsibility for a mother who is incapable of keeping her daughter safe and providing for her. At a very young age, Lena learns harsh lessons about her role in the world that caused her to rely more on herself than on others for her survival. Little Lena could not find her voice, perhaps driving her to express herself through performance a few years later.

Silence is an act of respectability if not a consequence of it. Respectability is expected of Horne as the granddaughter of Cora Calhoun Horne. She concludes, I was born into "the world of the Negro middle class. Our family, I find, followed most of the patterns that sociologists—those who have studied the so-called black bourgeoisie have found were common to our class . . . We were a family of readers and playgoers."[3] Of her matriarchal grandmother, Calhoun Horne, she says, "She was very proud of her feet which were small and perfectly shaped and she always wore fabulous shoes."[4] In other words, appearances were important. Such thinking led her grandmother to stay married to a man that she rarely spoke to at home. Horne's paternal grandmother put her energy into advancing the race by focusing on educating the Black working class and engaging in civil rights issues—activities that were commonly championed among the Negro middle class, particularly Black women, of the period. Horne would later learn that her grandmother was "active with the Urban League and the NAACP (National Association for the Advancement of Colored People), the Suffragette movement and all kinds of social-work activity."[5] Actor and activist Paul Robeson, whom Horne would later befriend, informed her that her grandmother chased him off the corners and later helped him to "get a scholarship at Rutgers."[6] For Horne herself, this meant that her conservative grandmother prepared her for how to at least perform respectability to advance the race. Middle-class Black people like her grandmother were always watching and judging.

If her grandmother was fond of performing in public, so was her mother. A hopeful actress herself, Edna Scottron had a major influence on her only child. By the time Lena was two years old, Edna and the girl's father had separated and both abandoned little Lena to live with her grandmother. Unable to withstand the tense relationship she had with her mother-in-law, Scottron left to pursue a career in theater. In 1922, she was cast in an all-Black musical, *Dumb Luck*, which starred Ethel Waters and Alberta Hunter among three other cast members. Surviving for only two nights, the short-lived experience would whet her acting appetite. About four years later, when little Lena was about six, Edna resurfaced, disrupted her daughter's stable home life, and took her to the South where she moved from town to town hoping to build a career acting in the traveling vaudeville shows. However, in her autobiography, Horne obscured the reason for this movement, only stating that her mother looked for work. She was mysteriously absent for days. This silence prompts readers to consider what Horne's biographer, James Gavin, concludes, that the single woman most certainly had to resort to prostitution to care for her daughter. Referring to an unnamed source, Gavin states, "Lena would later observe that a black woman of the day was 'apt to be a whore' when times got rough. Since actresses were already deemed loose women, prostitution proved an easy segue."[7] He goes on, "A journalist who knew her well recalled her mentioning that Edna sold her body, at least briefly." It wasn't surprising; Horne also spoke of her mother's prostitute friends, with whom she'd stayed.[8] Striving for respectability could not necessarily protect a single Black woman in the South. Unable to get steady work, like many other Black women, she also took jobs as a salesperson, maid, or whatever else she could do.[9]

In the South, Lena became more aware of her body, from the color of her skin to her body as an object of desire. She was called

"Yaller! Yaller!" and the color of her skin was a mark of shame as far as the children had been taught. She recalled that they chanted, "Got a white daddy! Shame! Shame!" then danced around her and referred to her as a "little yellow bastard."[10] Her family's visible history of European ancestry served to marginalize her in a community where she was foreign, not only because of the color of her skin but also because of her New York accent. Unkowledgeable of racial history, the children charged Lena as being the result of a sin, an object of scorn. In retrospect, Horne understood the reason for the treatment and tried to translate it to her audience: "To some Negroes light color was far from being a status symbol; in fact, it's quite the opposite. It is evidence that your lineage has been corrupted by white people."[11] Almost as a recurring theme, *Lena* shows her resisting corruption.

Her body as a narrative of shame would become a repetitive refrain in her life's story. Neither her mother nor her father was present to protect her from the dangers that a girl alone may have to endure. Shifting from a specific personal "I" to an unidentified "you," Horne strongly suggests that an older man with whom she was left sexually abused her: "Back in Macon, those good women had told me; Don't be a bad girl. Don't let a boy touch you."[12] If respectability could not keep her mother from resorting to prostitution to pay the bills, it could not protect her daughter from a pedophile. She reflected, "you haven't been told whether you're to blame or it's the other person's fault. All you know is that if somebody touches you it's bad."[13] She expresses yet another example when silence or not telling is associated with respectable practices. How she dealt with the contradictions of being a Black girl who was expected to uphold respectability in a society that did not treat Black girls or women as respectable would be a question she would grapple with throughout her career. To be sure, as a performer she was constantly under scrutiny.

Dealing with the scrutiny of people in public spaces became a way of life when she worked at Harlem's famous Cotton Club, a segregated club for White patrons that featured Duke Ellington's and Cab Calloway's bands. According to Horne, her mother, who had by then married a White Cuban man, arranged for her to have an audition, and she agreed with hopes that she could bring money into a family that was suffering greatly from the Depression. At the age of sixteen, the Cotton Club became the place where she would learn how to hone her craft as a dancer, singer, and aspiring actress. Through a series of comments, she suggests that she had very little talent, but her looks made her of interest to the Cotton Club's management and perhaps for other jobs. In this sense, she acknowledges how her light skin gave her a privilege that other women may not have had despite their ability to do more than "carry a tune." Choosing a humble approach, Horne's tone expresses doubt in her abilities, "I could carry a tune, but I could hardly have been called a singer; I could, thanks to Anna Jones, dance a little, but I could hardly be called a dancer. I was tall and skinny and I had very little going for me except a pretty face and long, long hair that framed it rather nicely."[14] She also felt as though her look of respectability enhanced her marketability: "Also, I was young—about sixteen—and despite the sundry vicissitudes of my life, very, very innocent."[15] Horne's story is for a civil rights era audience who would have had an opinion, whether spoken aloud or not, about the importance of revering Black icons, especially Black women, based on their looks. Looking innocent was endearing.

However, the body sells, especially a light-skinned one. According to *Ebony* (a magazine for Black audiences), dancing ability had to be balanced with physical appearance: 1. Beauty 2. Height: 5'5" or more 3. Weight: 120 pounds or less 4. A little rhythm and knowledge of body movement 5. Age: Not over 26.[16] Gavin's choice of words speaks to the voyeuristic nature that Lena endured as a young dancer: "Throughout the show, one could ogle the finest flesh in Harlem: that of the Cotton Club girls, a line of smiling beauties who were billed as 'tall, tan, and terrific.' Hardly any were darker than café au lait."[17] For the White audience members were the "ones ogling," they enjoyed "the flesh" of young Black women. No matter how light the woman, any patron who came to the Cotton Club knew whoever was performing there may have been of a certain type, but also had talent among their peers. Horne was also aware that the oglers came for the purpose of fulfilling their desire for the Black exotic. As an object of their desire, Horne had strong words: "The most galling thing was that the club was owned by whites . . . who based their business on giving their white brethren a thrilling peek at the 'exotic' world of the Negro."[18] Moving from the business of gazing at the Black exotic, she expressed how she felt about the experience more personally, "I sensed that the white people in the audience saw nothing but my flesh, and its color."[19] For a girl who was also being told to guard herself from being touched and to be a "good girl," her line of work at such a young age revealed various kinds of threats to a Black female's body and especially one with European features. It also revealed the contradictions of a mother who insisted that she stay a virgin but encouraged her daughter to use her body to make money and build a career.

And for her part, Horne took deep pleasure in the work she was doing. It cannot be overlooked that as the White patrons may have indulged their desires to see Black girls dancing and Black jazz men playing, the performers also had an opportunity to embrace their pleasure. Surely Horne showed promise when she auditioned at fifteen years old. The Cotton Club, as Horne described it, was "a remarkable institution," renowned for presenting the best of Black entertainers.[20] Her assessment of her self as a good-looking body expresses how she may have been conditioned to think of her ability at the time, especially given the fact that there was competition among the community of performers. During this time, she worked diligently to develop her skills. She practiced her dancing skills, enjoyed the attention she got from the hustlers who knew her wayward father, and seized opportunities to take the spotlight. Horne can be found in Cotton Club film shorts exposing a "radiant smile" and "moving much more capably than she ever admitted she could."[21] Indeed, Horne's narrative voice muted how she made conscious efforts to move up in the business and suggests, instead, she presented her success as happening by happenstance. While still a teenager, she landed a singing part alongside bandleader Jimmie Lunceford in the Cotton

Club Parade in 1934. Of those years, she possessed fond memories. Horne proclaimed, "At sixteen, I was inexhaustible, and if I did not see the Cotton Club as a stepping stone to a much larger career, and if there were a good many distasteful aspects to life in the club, I was still enough of a stage-struck kid to take some pride and pleasure in associating with the great talents who played the club."[22]

Horne came to understand the unevenness of her life at an early age. She performed an "exotic, wonderful, rhythmic, happy-go-lucky persona on stage," but lived in a "roach infested tenement." At work, the performers received low wages that hardly properly compensated for the number of shows they did at a segregated facility that provided no bathrooms for its dancers (their only option was to use a basin). Yet, during this time of her life, she learned to find pleasure in a personal space where it could not be disturbed by others. Through performance, she could escape, close her eyes, and enjoy the "pride and pleasure" of her body.

Lost in her increasing need to be self-reliant is the question of identity as a maturing girl who was influenced by a Black grandmother who espoused respectability in her community work. Society, as Horne makes clear, had an expectation that she would maintain her dignity by adhering to the standards of respectability. As such, questions about sexual agency are not asked or answered. Her mother, like so many mothers, did what she could to preserve her daughter's purity. She and her hot-tempered husband stood guard at the Cotton Club where the young girl worked and toured with young Lena to ensure that she was not harmed by any of the men that she encountered. She saw their presence as somewhat unnecessary given her experience and lack of interest in sex, but she may have underestimated the necessity of their presence for they were not just concerned about her explorations of sexual curiosity but must also have been concerned of the wantonness of the older men as well. What she found problematic was that there was no communication, a secrecy by which she was unable to circumvent. What should she do about the hormonal urges that she had? There was no one to pose this question to, and its lack of attention pushed her toward a marriage that she thought, in fact hoped, would offer a compromise between her sexual curiosity and her interest in upholding respectable standards, at least in public.

Answering the question would lead her to marry the light-skinned son of a preacher in 1937 who gave her the attention that appealed to her budding womanhood. Louis Jones was a man that she said could never reconcile how his education could not overcome racial limits. He was unhappy with the fact that he could only work a menial job in an office. His way to find pleasure, as far as Horne could see, was to buy things with money they did not have. Creditors would haunt their marriage and so would his anger and resentment. Yet, they had two children in the midst of their misery. Noticeably, Horne did not characterize their marriage as one that was joined by love; rather, it was an opportunity for her to be "set free."[23] In other words, it was an opportunity for her to have sex within respectable confining standards—if not with a preacher then with a preacher's son. Horne sought marriage for two reasons. On one hand, she was hoping to "use Louis . . . to run away from a life that she did not want."[24] On the other hand, she wanted to have sex without feeling shame for her desire. Although she was not aware of her intentions, in retrospect she gained awareness. Horne writes, "I also realize now that I could have been talked out of that marriage. To put it bluntly, I was still a virgin and one of the reasons marriage was so attractive to me was that I was desperately eager to know the physical side of love."[25] At the age of forty-eight, Horne used the autobiography to freely speak her truth in a way that counters the truth that had been kept from her about how to confront and manage her sexual desires. She goes on to condemn secrecy that is rooted in the politics of respectability, "If someone had simply told me to go to bed with Louis, or with some other nice boy, a great deal of the pressure that simple curiosity can generate would have worked for me."[26] Horne was looking for pleasure in a world that saw indulging sexual pleasure as an excess. Without question, their marriage, at least for Horne, was a joining of a young woman who wanted to satisfy her sexual urgencies and who wanted to escape the demanding life of performance with a willing partner. Eventually, what would save her from the marriage was her first and true love—performance.

Under the cloak of performance, Horne's existence as a public persona was essential to survival. She had begun to build a following as a woman with a voice and a beautiful face. In *Lena*, she reveals little of how she felt about her looks, but she often speaks about her voice. More specifically, the process of developing a voice as part of her public identity if not also part of her private one is prevalent in this section of the autobiography. From the attention that she dedicates to developing her voice skills, readers might surmise that the voice itself—her attempts to understand her weaknesses and strength, her love of her voice in contrast to her respect for other Black female singers—is a metaphor for her maturation into her womanly self. First, she has no mentor or voice coach. So little did she know about how to preserve her voice, she would often find herself hoarse after belting out tunes in cabarets and clubs. Her lack of a performance coach may draw us to the lack of a consistent mother figure in her life. If the question of how to preserve her voice is not answered, neither is the question of how to preserve her body and reputation in the name of respectability.

As a performer, rather early into her career, a manager tried to teach her to sing like Ethel Waters, a versatile singer who had established a reputation for her soulful blues renditions. Once Horne realized what was happening and resisted, she used her voice to ask the most important question of her career and maybe of her life: "Who am I?" In other words, how can she feel the pleasure of singing and know that she is singing as herself? This part of the journey would include finding songs that she felt comfortable singing. She does not share why certain songs are chosen and others are not, but her last album contains some of those read as an accompaniment to the autobiography *Being Myself*.

As she began to define herself as a singer, she would have to do the same in film. For those who could afford it, seeing a film was a distraction from the problems of society. Perhaps more than any other representation of a racialized Black body, the Black mulatta performer becomes pornographic. Black feminism, observes Nash, "has often read visual culture's treatment of black women even in nonpornographic texts as a kind of pornography; pornography has become both a rhetorical device and an analytical framework, a strategy for describing and critiquing a particular re-presentation of black women's bodies."[27] Pornographic representations become escapes for the voyeur. Duke, the protagonist of *The Duke Is Tops*, addresses what the voyeur misses to an audience of Black people: "As I look over your smiling faces, the thought comes to me that a lot of those smiles may be covering up sickness and suffering." Duke's successful attempt to sell an elixir that will solve the problems of poor Black people's troubles, sickness, and suffering speaks to the pleasure of watching film. Observers seek an escape from reality that satisfies a personal desire. Yet, the emotions that are experienced merely cover up the reality the person is seeking to escape. A Black woman, in this case, the beautiful mulatta as object of the observer, allows the observer to indulge a desire of whatever the observer associated with her, for example, sexual desire, trauma, pain, vulnerability. Horne learned to maneuver within this complex space.

Although known for her sultry voice and beautiful looks, Horne mostly had supporting roles throughout her film career. Her debut film, *The Duke Is Tops* (1938), written by Phil Dunham and Ralph Cooper (Duke), is about a show producer, Duke (Ralph Cooper), who is in love with a star singer, Ethel Andrews (Lena Horne). Duke's talent is his ability to organize and coordinate Black talent—dancers, singers, bands—for theater owners, and when the film begins we learn that he has used his own money to produce the show with Ethel as the star. When he is approached by two men with connections to New York to let Ethel go with them, she rebuffs the idea. Motivated by the men who tell him he needs to think of Ethel and not himself, he reminds her that she is under contract; this severs their working and romantic relationships. Unable to make money from the show without her, Duke finds himself teaming up with a charlatan that calls himself a "doctor" and organizes a traveling medical show with the purpose of selling an elixir to Black folks in small towns that can cure anything. But, when he learns from a radio show that Ethel's luck has run out in the business because, as a White sponsor says, "She's a specialty, not a star," he abruptly leaves the traveling show, and rushes to her in New York just as she has announced plans to her friend to return to Alabama. They reunite and Duke coordinates a new show starring Ethel. The film ends after the show and a kiss between Ethel and Duke. Ultimately, it is a story about Black people's pursuit of pleasure and the pleasure that Ethel experiences is as much about her ability to sing as it is about their relationship.

Although limited in character development, her character possesses admirable feminist qualities, which are likely unintentional. Men dominate the film and, as a result, we learn about Ethel's worth from the men. They determine that she "has what it takes" and it is they that orchestrate her move from Alabama to New York. Consequently, they have great influence over her career, including where she lives. Duke's initial refusal to separate from Ethel is because of his role in advancing her career. He reasons to the men, "I studied Ethel. Taught her. Brought out the best in her." So limited is her role in the film, we have no way of knowing anything about how she developed her ability to sing and perform in front of audiences, but what we can surmise is that the money Duke uses to front the show is from profits he makes from her talent and willingness to perform for his material pleasure. This becomes abundantly clear when she asks him, "That's all I mean to you, dollars and cents?" Ethel challenges any perspective that she is a commodity that is for sale. Despite his heroic act of pretending to sell the rights of her performance to another man, he suffers from her absence. Further, so do the other performers and stage manager. All of them depend on Ethel's desire to perform and to do it with Duke as her partner.

Women do not comment on Ethel's performance. Her friend, Ella (Neva Peoples), is the only other woman in the film and her role is to see what Ethel cannot. She is a brown woman in contrast to Ethel and her role in the film is to assist Ethel and to advise. When she learns that Duke wrote the check for $5,000 that he says has come from the manager he has sold her contract to, she acquiesces to Duke's plea not to tell Ethel for her own good. Later, after she tells Ethel the truth, she says that she has been told she is a "cyclist" (meaning a psychic) and then Duke appears at the door. Her ability to see what is going on and the possibility of what is to come places her in a position to put others first. Nefarious, villainous reasons do not inspire her choices in a business where there are such few choices for women. In fact, by telling her friend the truth, she frees Ethel to choose and, as a result, Ethel pursues pleasure how she pleases.

Ethel is representative of the Black women, including Horne, who dared to see where their talent could take them. She rightfully enjoys mobility, a measure of freedom. Initially, she chooses to remain with Duke and only leaves him when she believes that her only value to him is the ability to make money. Ethel's choices are to stay with her lover, Duke, or to move on without him. His absence—his presumed selling of her—does not deter her from moving to New York to pursue her love of performance. It is her inability to satisfy White men that disrupts her willingness to try to move from a small traveling show to a prominent White-owned establishment in New York. Although it was filmed in Hollywood, the low-budget film with the thin, underdeveloped plot does show the challenges of Black performers who boldly defined their successes by crossing racial lines in the entertainment industry.

Ethel's attempt to possess pleasure outside her working and romantic relationship with Duke requires that the public must also feel a semblance of pleasure. For performers, this results in capturing the critical eye of White men who invest in how they feel about the movements of the light-skin body. There is a price, however. She becomes subject to the whims of White men. Her success is determined by the amount of money they make and how she makes them feel. Director William Nolte isolates her as she sings on a stage alone. Her position in the spotlight calls to viewers to also consider the position of vulnerability she is in as her body is surveilled by strangers in a segregated club. Horne knew this experience well, but Ethel is for the first time separated from her community of performers, the other Black singers and dancers whom she previously knew and traveled with. Duke, who is cast as her protector and supporter, is not there to run interference between Ethel and any attempts to violate her. As she sings, the White men look on and register their emotional response by clapping and smiling. How they feel and how she looks prompts them to invest more money in continuing their feelings of pleasure, inspiring them to move her into a starring position. Duke sees this as an accomplishment for Ethel when he reads the cover of *Variety* newspaper that praises the "Bronze Nightingale." "I knew you could do it," muses Duke. The film illuminates an example of how Black women's attempts to seize pleasure require them to give in order to take. Ethel must give of herself—her safety, her lover—to enjoy the pleasure of receiving compensation to sing. This is the risk of movement, the transformation that often leads to pleasure.

Pleasure, ultimately, is hers. Without hesitation, she tells Ella that she will return to the South. That choice is as much hers as it is when she decides to return to Duke's employ when he reenters her life to restart the show. Singing the lyrics to her last song, "I don't care what people say, we stay together" is an expression of resistance to Duke's willingness to succumb to people in the industry who may wish to separate the two. He is an object of her pleasure just as much as singing.

It was, as Horne clarifies, a performance. She writes, "Making the picture was no fun."[28] Her description of the film does not accurately capture the plotline, as she says that Ethel and Duke, "kept splitting up and reconciling throughout the film," when, in fact, they split up only once and most of the action takes place between that split and the time that they reconcile. Through her dismissal of the film as "innocuous" and not "an important picture," she raises herself above the fact that the "plot was just an excuse to string a lot of song-and-dance numbers together."[29] Despite the problems of the plot, she found achievement in her work: "I had a couple of numbers to do, including one called, 'I Know You Remember' that a couple of critics eventually singled out as best in the picture."[30] Notably, she did not remember the plot, but recalls the critics' reactions. It is this "singling out as best" that she chooses to spotlight in her life's story. Nevertheless, the critics' recognition gave her the assurance she needed to continue as a performer, and perhaps made her separation from her family, including a newborn baby girl, worth the sacrifice.

Escaping the misery of her marriage, Horne took an opportunity to have a potentially pleasurable experience. Just a few months after giving birth to her first child, when she received the call from Harold Gumm, an agent working with Ralph Cooper, a handsome light-skinned actor known for his work as an emcee at the Apollo Theater in Harlem, she was hardly ready for her first leading role. Horne was known for being beautiful and rather slim; her post-pregnancy body had left her chubbier than Cooper expected when she arrived for filming. Her "wide-eyed wonderment," according to Gavin, made her a nonthreatening presence to the women who had more experience working at movie studios. As a result, they welcomed her, Horne recalls. Gavin refutes her autobiographical persona's perspective that filming was "no fun," instead noting that members of the cast concluded she "she seemed to be having a ball, both on the set and in the California sunshine."[31] As a new mother, it is likely that she was conflicted—by feeling happy about the opportunity and the potential for her career and guilty for leaving her family for the ten days it took to shoot the film in Los Angeles. In Gavin's estimation, "her singing is generic, her acting flat. But she conveys a high-class image."[32] The latter is what was most important for the newly wedded mother, the wife of a preacher's son whose father didn't attend the wedding because he considered women of her profession to be whores. It would be an image she maintained.

Horne recognized that she was more than a wife and mother, and performing allowed her to embrace that other self. Married Lena, a new mother, needed "fun"; she would come to understand there was a line between her acting and the business of acting. In other words, an experience of pleasure on film does not necessarily extend to the experience of being a part of the filming process. One of her reasons for agreeing to leave her infant daughter was the promise of payment. Once she arrived, she found that the producers "were paying off in promises of what she would make later."[33] Cooper, like Duke, could never pay his actors what he promised. Another reason she left her family was to put distance between herself and the troubled marriage she had rushed into. Understandably, her husband was angered by the lack of money.

Indeed, pleasure came at a cost. Yet, the experience introduced her to a larger audience and revived the career that she had left behind. Despite her interest in having a life outside of show business, performing was her first love, even though she did not enjoy the business of performance. According to Horne, she was "forbidden" by her husband to attend the premiere of the film in Pittsburg, which had the effect of also offending the NAACP, a civil rights organization that had high expectations of her. For her husband, Horne felt that he believed he had "rescued me from a life of sin."[34] Although she did not attend the NAACP's premiere of the film, the organization's attention to it gave her approval among bourgeois Blacks. Accolade, like performance, was exclusively hers. It could not be shared with her husband whom she sensed resented the immense pleasure she enjoyed in being a performer. And, perhaps, since he was not the object of that pleasure, he hoped to keep her with him at home.

After her separation from her husband, she returned to building her career and navigating the industry. As her popularity grew, she certainly became aware of how she fed the pleasures Nash identifies as, "pleasures in looking, pleasures in being looked at, pleasures in performing racial fictions, pleasures in upending racial fictions of the industry's moguls."[35] Filming *Cabin in the Sky* in 1943 was more of a challenge for Horne. In her autobiography, she says that, despite a foot injury, she "had fun" playing the role of a jezebel character who is a seductive pawn of the devil. It was a role in which she took deep pleasure. Noticeably, she gives more attention to filming *Cabin* than any of her other films. Cast opposite Ethel Waters, who plays religious, upright Petunia, and Eddie "Rochester" Anderson, Petunia's hard-headed husband, Joe, *Cabin* moves in and out of a love story, a musical, and a religious revival.

It begins with a discussion among church leaders and their optimism about the gambler Little Joe, who is married to the faithful churchgoing, fervently praying Petunia. Little Joe's reluctance to go to the front of the church and rededicate his life to Christ sends him to a club where he is shot and nearly dies. But for Petunia's pleading with God to not take the love of her life, Little Joe would be taken to hell where Lucifer's son is waiting. Joe is given a chance to return to his life, change his ways, and receive redemption in heaven if he would only stop gambling and stay away from Georgia Brown (played by Lena Horne). During what is revealed as a long dream sequence that Joe has while recuperating from his injury, he wins the sweepstakes, takes up with Georgia Brown, is fatally shot along with Petunia, and, with Petunia's help, is granted entry into heaven. After their happy ending, Joe awakens and tells Petunia to throw away his sweepstakes tickets so as to not tempt fate.

Viewers may assume that his rejection of the ticket is ultimately a rejection of the lifestyle that included all forms of temptation, including the gorgeous Georgia Brown. Horne came to this project as a woman who had been taught to be a woman quite the opposite of this role. She had been told by one of her male peers to be "a lady—not a whore and don't be treated like one."[36] To perform a jezebel, then, gave her a kind of pleasure in the act of indulging the thing she was not to be and that her father-in-law concluded that she was. This is a clear act of independence and rebellion against the voyeuristic critic. She shares, "I was enjoying myself hugely on this picture. For the first time I had a real role to play and for the first time I felt myself to be an important part of the whole enterprise, not just a stranger who came in for a few days to do a song or two."[37] By proclaiming that she enjoyed playing the role, she is also unapologetic in embracing a stereotype rather than finding shame in it as she was taught to feel by the children of her youth. Indeed, the role is significantly different than the naive girl she played in the *The Duke Is Tops*. In this role advancements were made because of her presence, "the cameraman finally decided they liked the way I photographed and the make-up people finally invented a shade for me that didn't make me look like Al Jolson doing 'Mammy.'" Here, about five years after filming *Duke* she is an influencer and not the influenced.

What is most striking is the attention that is given to her body, her looks, and her movements that do not rely on musical performances. In her first scene, she enters and there is a multifocal lens that examines and scrutinizes her—first is the film's audience, the second is Lucifer's son, and the third is Georgia herself. She moves straight to a mirror and admires herself. Rather than to hear her voice, what she admires about her face is narrated by Lucifer as her thoughts of pride and narcissism. In her mind she hears how beautiful she is and wonders how Little Joe, presumably her former lover, is doing. She then saunters over to a dressing area and disrobes. With her back turned to the camera, she is seen from the side fully covered from the waist down, but her top half is covered in only a bra until she puts on a short-cut blouse.

Georgia Brown, as the characters often refer to her with guttural emphasis, is introduced into the narrative before she is seen (italics mine). Therefore, what we see is what we expect to see through the perspective of the heavenly soldier of God, Lucifer's son, and Little Joe. While the heavenly soldier and Lucifer's son are battling over the rights to Joe's soul, Lucifer cuts in, "Just wait until your boss starts checking up on his carryin' on with Georgia Brown." Acknowledging his indiscretions, Joe looks down and Lucifer goes on, "She's my pappy's favorite child." Indeed, Georgia is welcomed by the harem of devils as one of their agents. She is akin to evil, and Joe's marriage to Petunia is jeopardized by his attraction to the lascivious wiles of Georgia Brown.

After not seeing Joe for a while, she yields to the temptations of her own spirit that have been stoked by Lucifer's son and goes to Joe's job. There she does not find him, but she is put in the path of a telegram that informs him he has won money. Taking this news as a perfect opportunity to visit him at the house he shares with the hard-working, God-fearing Petunia, she saunters over and gives him her full attention. Horne plays the role of the seductress convincingly. She takes off her hat and places a large, presumably fragrant, flower in her hair. Little Joe is asleep in a hammock outside, and this scenario may draw viewers' memories to an Eve scenario. She leans over the fence to which the hammock is tied and says, "Hello, Little Joe." Not only is she dressed provocatively in the blouse tied around her narrow waist, but she has no problem moving into his space, touching him, and not taking no for an answer. The more he resists her, the more effort she puts into getting his attention. At some point, she puts her foot on the arm of the chair he is sitting in; the fact that she is wearing a skirt only intensifies the sexual energy she is trying to stir. She places her hand on his face to get him to pay close attention to her. Joe admits that he "has been trying his best not to think of her lately" and she, armed with the knowledge, smiles and says, "Why would you want to forget me, Sugar?" Finally, she makes her move and sits on his lap and he kisses her. Joe sings about the folly of consequences and Georgia sings, the only song she has to sing in the film, about consequences not being a problem: "Who's scared of consequences?" She sings through a toothy, seductive smile.

Georgia went there to get Joe and if her body will not fully distract him, then the news of the sweepstakes winnings (proverbial forbidden fruit) does. When Petunia comes in medias res and hears Joe promise to buy Georgia a diamond ring and a club, she does not know that he is merely rewarding her for giving him the news and that he is not trying to woo her. However, Petunia's act of banishing him seals the deal that Georgia was offering. When next we see the three, they are in a club. Georgia and Little Joe enter dressed to the nines and Georgia is donning big, bright jewelry much to the delight of the club goers. They know that she is being taken care of by Little Joe, whom the people are also glad to see. A request comes from one of them for Georgia to perform and she is placed on the piano. Little Joe reminds her that she is supposed to be a lady. Ironically, he seems to have forgotten that she is in a relationship with him—a man who is probably still married. Joe's proclamation reminds the film's audience that women are judged as either being ladies or not being ladies. For Georgia, she is either respectable or not. Enjoying the attention of others, especially men, may jeopardize her as they can determine to which category she belongs. The fast life among gamblers and partiers is clearly the lifestyle that each has embraced and has taken pleasure in. There is no safety in such pleasures as it leaves them vulnerable to tragedy.

Georgia's allure is her power over Little Joe, but her sexuality does not supersede love. Petunia's entrance into the space of people she would normally see as lowlifes and in need of God's redemption shows not only the pain she carries after losing the love of her life but also her willingness to go to him under the pretense of wanting half the money he won. Georgia begins to lose the spotlight. The audience sees her movements more than it hears her desire for him to remain at her side. As he looks at Petunia dancing and then hears her cries for help to be rescued from his nemesis, Georgia Brown hooks her arm around his neck. Her act is useless, as he wrests loose and is eventually shot for his heroism. Joe's redemption and entrance into heaven only occurs because Georgia repented and gave her possessions to a church. Again, we see that the seductive temptress holds power over the fate of the man whose faults may send him into the clutches of hell. Unlike many films, especially of the period that saw men in positions of power, this would be the one film in Horne's career that gave her an opportunity to play a role that placed her in a position of power over a man—whether for good or for bad.

As the granddaughter of an activist, Horne began to see the power of her presence in the industry. Kirsten Pullen, like many scholars, has seen her as being "doomed" by history: "Horne's Hollywood persona negotiated [an] ambivalent racial and sexual inheritance by casting Horne as the pure but doomed tragic mulatto from the minstrel stage, separating her from the sexualized blues women or grotesque comic figures."[38] On the contrary, I argue that Horne learned how to own her image for her own gratification as a performer and then as a member of the race. Walter White of the NAACP was instrumental in molding her as an "uplifting symbol of the Negro race through the silver screen."[39] Horne was a rare sight in Hollywood—she was a Black woman who in 1942 received an MGM contract; therefore, she chose her roles wisely. What more could she dream of? Although she had this distinguished position, being under contract meant that she had to deal with any number of restrictions. A contracted actor with one studio had to get permission to work with another. Major studios almost exclusively hired Whites to direct films and act as crewmen, making few roles for the few Black women who were marketable to their targeted audience. Commenting on the importance of her position, Kwakiutl L. Dreher observes, "Horne's arrival on MGM's studio lot in 1942 paves the way for a new representation of Negro womanhood to supplant Hattie McDaniel's mammy figure."[40] What roles were available for Black people involved singing and dancing. For women, they were in subordinate, supportive roles. For the most part, they responded to the actions of men.

Just as with *The Duke Is Tops* and *Cabin in the Sky*, the decisions that Horne's characters make depends on the action of a man, but she had presence in these roles. At the age of twenty-six she was placed opposite significantly older men (a common practice among the casting of all young actresses then and now), as she was in *Stormy Weather* (1943), a film that closely parody's the career of renowned tap dancer Bill Williamson, played by Bill "Bojangles" Robinson. Among other roles, Robinson was known as having been cast as a dancer opposite Shirley Temple, a popular White child actress. *Stormy Weather* would be the first major role he had and the first and only as a love interest. By the time the film was released, audiences would have known the song "Stormy Weather." It had been made popular by Ethel Waters. For the most part, the song is about a woman who has the blues, a result of her man leaving her "heavy-hearted and sad." In a spectacular ending scene in a sequence of high energy, well-choreographed performances by the best known in the business, Horne sings the song about her breakup with Bill. Horne's performance as Selina has been seen as reserved. Pullen observes, "Her character performances as well as specialty numbers solidified Horne's aloof, contained, reserved performance style, which both Horne and her audiences associated with her 'authentic' self."[41] However, Horne's acceptance of this role not only speaks to her conscious activism as an icon but also expresses one of the many selves she portrayed in film. Indeed, Selina's assertion of her place in the industry and her final choice of marriage represents moments when she, like many women, negotiated their needs and wants.

Stormy Weather's action takes place during the interwar era, beginning with Bill and his friends' return from performing with a Black regiment in World War I. When the film begins, Selina has a job as a club performer. Her accompanist is Chick Bailey (Emmet "Babe" Wallace), who is discussed before he enters the action of the film. The film slowly unfolds the fact that Selina is a confident up-and-coming star. Bill knows her only as the younger sister of a friend who died in the war. Like Horne's other two films, *Stormy Weather* emphasizes a voyeuristic element of her presence. Even when she is not in front of an audience, she is being observed by Bill. When he enters the nightclub and sees her for the first time, he is visibly enamored by her, and he is not the only one. She is seen dressed in brightly colored clothes that stand out in the crowd of men who reach out to her for a touch of her hand. Bill's face lights up when he sees Selina and he exclaims to his friend from the regiment, Gabe, "Look at that gal standing over there." If it is not true for Horne, it is certainly true for Selina—her career relies heavily on people looking at her and liking what they see. Without knowing who she is, the audience's first glimpse is an introduction to a woman deemed as important, among Black men, at least.

Selina seems aware that she is not just a performer and has a certain level of understanding about the power she holds over herself and her ability to advance the career of others. When she and Bill meet, as with these race films, it is not long before the conversation is interrupted by a dance number. The dance scene seems like a teaser, a glimpse at what will come in the thin development of their romance and the next scene that will feature them dancing together. In an earlier conversation, it is revealed to the audience that she is highly regarded for her skills. An older mentor tells her, "I hear that you're a big star now." In fact, Selina is a partner, as she makes clear when she introduces Chick Bailey to the table. Gabe's lies that he is like brothers with Chick may entertain the woman he is trying to impress with his nonexistent riches and lack of agent's skills, but it is Selina who consistently unmasks him for her own entertainment. Chick's entrance into a conversation in which he has been both validated as a respected leader and claimed by a man he has never met gives Selina an opportunity to show, through her connection with Chick, that she too has influence in the industry.

Gabe's lies are interrupted by Selina's call to perform with Chick as her accompanist. In the spotlight the audience sees her for a second time in isolation, but this time she is doing the work she is known and admired for—singing. As she sings and Chick, dressed in a tuxedo and seated at a grand piano, plays, the spotlight shifts from him to her and follows her movement from one end of the piano to the other. Selina, Lena Horne's alter ego, knows how to command her audience to follow her. In fact, Horne's skills as a singer had grown considerably since *The Duke Is Tops*. Utilizing strong command of her vocals, her voice is strong and mature. Her look, too, is sophisticated and accented appropriately by her flowing dress. Whether it is a directive from the director or Horne's choice, she does not look at the camera as she sings, keeping her character present within the performance of the character rather than moving outside the filming to connect with the real audience of the film.

In fact, singing "Stormy Weather" proved a major challenge for Horne. In an interview years later, she confessed that she was "terrified" to sing it because it was known as "Ethel's."[42] Indeed, Ethel Water's soulful rendition of the song was well known. But Horne was the star of a film and it was up to her to make the song her own. She finally found inspiration from her friend Cab Calloway who "whispered two words in her ear." It would turn out that those words were: Ethel Waters.[43] The result was a heartfelt rendition that became an iconic moment in her film career.

It is by no coincidence that Selina is a commanding performer. She tells Bill, who compliments her on her skills, that she is no accidental artist: "I practiced and studied. I have always been ambitious, haven't you Bill?" While the film is usually seen as being inspired by the career of Bill Robinson, it seems also inspired by Lena Horne and perhaps other Black women performers, such as Ethel Waters and Katherine Dunham who "practiced and studied" to build their careers. Certainly Robinson, who too was near the end of his career and life, was ambitious as he started his dancing career when a child. Bill retorts that he never has, but "sees things different now." By seeing Selina's success, Bill hopes for his own. Selina, then, is given the honor of being a model to the man whose return to the United States from France will leave him searching for a place where he can be a successful performer.

Their next performance together shows how well the two worked as performance partners. In this case, it is the cakewalk, a dance that became popular among enslaved people that involved high stepping as a form to mimic their owners. The Dunham dancers high step down stairs that wind around an elaborate cake. A call for all to join or a call to the community allows the two to take center stage where the dancers also turn their attention to Bill and Selina. In doing so, the dancers, as symbolic of community, acknowledge them as the community's pride. Robinson and Horne are also representative of the twentieth-century generation who may be aware of the dance of the enslaved, but who, in their modern dress and more modern dance, literally and figuratively move beyond the past. It is during this dance that she declares her ambition, giving her the power and platform to transform the industry from one that simply regurgitates stereotypes.

Next, following a time lapse, as Bill makes his way through the South trying to build his dancing and acting career, he finds himself taking menial jobs that provide him with his necessities. Ambition has taken Selina on the road with Chick, who is revered for building shows with people he meets and, more importantly, paying his performers. When Selina and Chick enter a restaurant where Bill is working, the man's face lights up at the sight of her.

However, Selina does not see Bill. One reason may be that she is not looking for him. The man who speaks to her is a waiter and she issues him a command, "hang it up," in reference to her mink coat. Selina sits in the Black-owned café of Memphis's Beale Street and listens happily to Fats Waller and Ada Brown. Her light arms and shoulders are bare and she is dressed in an elaborate outfit. In fact, she speaks little in the scene; her body communicates a level of seduction that is irresistible to Bill. When he comes to the table, she acknowledges that she recognizes him and communicates rather loudly through the widening of her eyes and movement of her shoulders. Rather than allow him to say that he is Bill in response to her question, she says that of course he is. Learning that he has no job as a performer, she asks Chick to give him a role in their show and Chick does, reluctantly. Selina uses her voice to support Bill's aspirations and Horne uses her body to communicate her power of influence as an attractive woman in a significant role.

Selina remains consistent about her career aspirations and her identity as an individual who does not feel obligated to take direction from a man. In fact, up until this point she makes requests to men and they respond with affirmation. Motivated by his jealousy of the attention she gives to Bill, Chick attempts to control her by saying he does not want any of his performers to be seen together in a sandwich shop. Selina firmly rejects his attempts to control her. In essence, he is trying to disrupt Bill's desire for her and her desire for Bill. Further, his method of doing this is placing restrictions on her movement. In a show of resistance, she tells Chick, "After the show is over I do what I please." After the next show, Bill knocks Chick out, and she takes pleasure in walking out on Bill's arm. Her smile and their carefree movement together gives them a sense of freedom motivated by each of their decisions.

Selina's liberation is rooted in how she feels about her work. There is something about being a performer that Bill, who wants to marry her, does not understand. Exhibiting masculine bravado at Chick's expense may suit her in the moment, but it cannot compare to the pleasure she takes from performing. Bill learns this when he shows her plans for a house and proposes that she quit the business and become a mother. During the conversation, she reminds him that they have had the conversation before and her answer is the same. Bill's counter that he thought she would respond differently because he had a contract with MGM and can pay for their needs means that he does not see the work that she does as a pleasure that she values as specifically hers. She tells him simply, the "house is not for us." And, that she does not "want" to settle down. Their exchange is representative of women's push for equality. By 1943, some women had the right to vote and more women were moving into the workplace because men were going off to war.

Bill says, "You can quit."

"Quit."

"Sure, you've worked long enough. It's time that you settle down. And we have a home and . . ."

"But Bill, I don't want to quit. I wouldn't be happy unless I went along with my work, just like you. Singing's in my blood."

"I'm sorry, Selina. I just thought maybe you'd see different now."

Selina walks away while saying, "Bill, I'll never see it differently. Never."

Selina is emphatic that she wants to work like Bill, but in fact does not acknowledge what she does as purely work. Although she receives pay for her artistic ability, she *wants* to sing. Singing is a part of her identity, and Bill's attempts to take her off the stage to domesticate her is something she will not consent to. Erin Chapman observes of women of the period, "New Negro women balance this expectation of men's patriarchal responsibility with a pragmatic acceptance of the overwhelming economic circumstances demanding their participation in the workforce and with a personal recognition of their own capabilities and needs."[44] Selina's response predates and nods to the feminist movement, but Horne's concern was the position of the race. Horne does not express how much she enjoyed being a performer as a part of her identity. Instead, she suppresses it and describes her career as something she came to by the pushing of her mother. At times, according to her, she enjoyed parts of her career. By contrast, Selina expresses her ambitious nature and delights in her ability to sing.

The final spectacular act is around the singing of "Stormy Weather." Katherine Dunham and her dancers support the singing with a memorable performance that begins in the background and then moves to the stage where Selina laments the loss of her lover. Horne is clear in her autobiography that she was not a blues singer. To sing "Stormy Weather" she thought was disingenuous, as she felt that she could not make people believe that she even knew what the blues was. In the film, it fits the plot. However, something is lost when the two reunite. As she looks in the direction of where Bill is seated, the film's audience may believe that Selina is sending him a message of pain in the best way she knows how. In between scenes, she tells him a woman can change her mind, suggesting that she will quit the business and go to the house with him that he had built with the hope that she would join him. Their last performance shows her coming out of the front door of a house dressed, probably, in white. The dress is long and her hat is round. Her look is a stark difference from the dark-colored dress she was wearing while singing "Stormy Weather." The couple is a celebration of domesticity and respectability. She is wearing heels, a fur stole, and a long dress complemented by Bill's tuxedo. These are the New Negroes America was introduced to nearly forty years earlier. In the end, Bill gets what he wants. We can only hope that Selina gets what she wants as well. More importantly, that whatever she has given up to be Bill's wife is what she wants to give up.

Stormy weather was a perfect way to describe Horne's personal life. She was embroiled in a tumultuous divorce with her estranged husband who had custody of their son. Her relationship with her son would never recover from their separation and what he may have emotionally processed as a result of being separated from both his mother and his sister. Notably, she found ways to separate herself from both pressures of performing and the problems of her marriage with men. Gavin notes, "her affairs may have represented an early stab of rebellion against [Walter] White and all those who sought to use her for their own means. Horne had goals unrelated to the NAACP."[45] Among these men were Joe Louis (who was married) and Orson Wells, but she was also known to have had a relationship with Louis B. Mayer, cofounder of Metro-Goldwin-Mayer. The latter affair was not well taken among some of her colleagues. Horne's choices in relationships show not only her willingness to take risks but also her bold intent to defy restrictions. She saw herself as important, and although it may have opened her to criticism from her colleagues and the NAACP, she would put few limits on pursuing her professional and personal desires.

Unlike Selina, Horne herself did not sacrifice her career or her sense of self to be a domestic, if for no other reason than the fact that she had financial obligations to her family. But, she also immensely enjoyed her work. She would continue to push social boundaries in her personal life. Four years after divorcing her first husband, in 1947 she quietly married Lennie Hayton, a White Jewish man, in France. Gavin notes that the Black press gave very little attention to the event once it was finally made public. The renowned Negro voyeur Langston Hughes, one of her many admirers, gave her signed copies of his books. Pursuing what gave her pleasure did not jeopardize her standing among the race she also wanted to please.

Horne's performative voice as a versatile, multitalented performer and autobiographer allows us to consider the relationship between the Black American experience of respectability and the suppression of pleasures. Her choices, as Chapman astutely observes, reflect how "New Negro women endeavored to define their sexual selves in the interstices between the one-dimensional identities their society imposed upon them."[46] In resistance to the suppression of Black women's desire to define pleasure, Horne learned how to use performance to define her self. She also rejected the negativity associated with her skin color by honing her skills and choosing roles that complicated the image of light-skinned Black women that continued to be promoted in film. Her ability to navigate the treacherous terrain of a largely segregated Hollywood found her embracing respectability, but not being confined by it. Horne does not deny that she did not have all the answers or always made the right decisions. However, through the ways she faced the challenges of Black womanhood we may applaud her for how she daringly identified and defined pleasure on her own terms.

3
Moms Mabley and the Art of Pleasure

I never will forget my granny. You know who hipped me, my great
grandmother. Her name was Harriet Smith. She lived in Brevard, NC.
This is the truth. She lived to be 118 years old. And you wonder why
Mom is hip today? Granny, hipped me. She said they lied to the rest
of them but I'm not going to let you be dumb. I'm going to tell you
the truth. They think they're telling me those pair of lies. Granny
tell me the truth about it. One day she was sitting out on the porch
and I said Granny how old does a woman get before she don't
want no more boyfriend? She was around 106 then. She said,
"I don't know, Honey. You'll have to ask someone older than me."
—"Grandma," *Best of Moms Mabley*

Although they may have known the same people in New York and
may have even crossed paths, Moms Mabley was distinctly different from the sex symbol Lena Horne. Yet, Mabley was, as Horne,
highly respected for her talents. By the time of Jackie "Moms"
Mabley's death in 1975, she had become known as the "Queen of
Comedy," a dominant force in the industry and respected artist
among her peers. She was an ambitious talent from North Carolina
and a product of the vaudeville circuit where she learned to
become a versatile entertainer who could captivate audiences with
tap dancing, singing, and joke-telling. Mabley was more than an
entertainer. She leveraged her pioneering presence on the comedy

stage to critique a repressive society that was especially limiting to Black women and even more so to Black queer women. Influenced by her southern upbringing, Mabley used comedy to move beyond socially restrictive boundaries.

Moms, as she came to be known in the industry, was born Loretta Mary Aiken in the late 1890s in Brevard, North Carolina. Brevard is a small town that grew from 350 in 1890 to 500 in 1896. The railroad, which was built in 1894, is credited with causing a steadily growing population and the expansion of facilities, such as the first brick commercial building in 1899.[1] Around the age of thirteen, after giving birth to two children, she left Brevard with a vaudeville show. Her career developed as a dancer with the famous duo Butterbeans and Susie, a show she joined in 1921. Under their tutelage and protection, she learned about show business and developed her skills. The pair reportedly brought her to New York in 1923 with encouragement that she should seek a career beyond the grueling circuit. In New York, she established a place for her alluring comedy identity on the stage and began to open for jazz luminaries such as Duke Ellington, Count Basie, and Cab Calloway.

This chapter is dedicated to looking at how Moms Mabley used the pleasure of comedy to challenge her growing audiences to question common perspectives of race, gender, and sexuality. Mabley used her voice to "educate" her audience about the problems of social restrictions that lead to suppression—more specifically, racial and gender stereotypes that limit progressive thinking, mistreatment of women and girls by older men, and sexual repression designed to privilege patriarchal heteronormativity. As exemplified in the epigraph, Mabley's comedic education in the South gave her access to a long tradition of comedy that taught her how to challenge her audience to move beyond restrictive spaces. Moving from the South to the North in search of a different and better life was a bold physical and mental move across boundaries. While Black women competed with one another to secure positions as actresses, singers, and dancers, Mabley competed with Black men to build her career as a stand-up comedienne. In this position, she had autonomy. First, she challenged her audience and her fellow comedians to reimagine the place of Black women in a socially restricted country as she gave them a glimpse of her idea of pleasure. Additionally, she showed her peers the importance of being herself beyond the audience's gaze. Ultimately, studying aspects of her life shows how a Black woman's choice to put her self first benefitted others.

Pleasure in comedy can be a form of defiance. By appealing to the hidden or silent desires of an audience, a comedienne, especially a Black comedienne, can say something that the audience member may be thinking but is too embarrassed to say aloud. In fact, depending on the era and location, saying something that may have been considered lewd or obscene could jeopardize the comedienne's freedom. Consider Moms saying, "There's nothing an old man can do for me but bring me a message from a young man." Expressing a preference for a younger man flips the tradition of the old man's preference for a young woman to the preference of an older woman. Audience members, especially women, can imagine themselves enjoying the experience of a younger lover and relive memories. The pleasure is hers as she enjoys the laughter and makes the declaration. Together, the comedienne and the audience enjoy mutual pleasure. However, there is more said here.

Comedy allows for expression as much as it does imaginative exploration. The comedienne leads the audience member on an excursion, an escape from a reality that may be depressing or sad, by manipulating language and the experiences of the audience to look at that experience from a different lens. Her repeated rejection of an older man causes the audience to wonder about the significance of the old man beyond the laughter, especially when she tells them that she was forced to marry one at a young age. Finding humor in situations where Black folks and women were exploited transformed them from victims of their social circumstances to empowered people with potential for advancement. Mabley would learn to make her audiences laugh at outrageously high rents, mistreatment of women and girls by older men, accidental or intentional death, growing old and useless, racial inequality, queer relationships, and other topics.

Moms Mabley's journey to the stage began in the South. Although Loretta Aiken left home at thirteen, she lived most of her childhood in the South, where she was influenced by Black southerners, especially talented Black women. Mabley would integrate what she learned from these women even as it differed significantly from blues women who in songs like Ma Rainey's "Deep Moaning Blues" ("Daddy, Daddy, please come home to me") longed for the love of a man or a woman. Instead, Mabley expressed no longing for a man or a woman. However, Aiken, who became known as Mabley, was more like the blues women than her performance may have portrayed. In her efforts to memorialize the life of Mabley, Clarice Taylor was one of the first Black performers to research the comedienne's life for a stage performance. From family members, she learned that Mabley had been raped by an older Black man when she was eleven years old and by a White sheriff two years later. Two babies, one by each man, were produced and given away for others to raise.[2] As a result of these births, biographers often write that she was raped twice, but there is no way to know how often her body was violated by these older men. There appear to be no interviews on record of these occurrences given by Mabley herself, but she may have been united with these two children later and had four others. What is clear is that she was not safe in her southern hometown after her father's sudden death. Reportedly her father, a volunteer firefighter, died instantly when his truck overturned on a curb while the unit was driving to an emergency in 1908. Young Loretta was about eleven years old at the time. James Aiken had been a successful entrepreneur who owned several businesses, including "a small bakery, the first barbershop for white people on Main Street, a drayage service, which transported mail from the railroad depot to the post office, and the most popular store-café which sold general merchandise, staples, and fancy groceries."[3] To date, Elise A. Williams, with the assistance of Mabley's family members, is the only scholar to have written an extensive study on Mabley's life and work.

Probably to save her granddaughter from further harm, Mabley's grandmother, Jane Aiken Hall, advised her to "put God in front," prompting her to leave Brevard to pursue a new life. Williams finds that the elder Aiken, whom Mabley referenced in her act as "hipping her," lived to be 104 years old, according to Brevard's *Transylvania Times*. Loretta Aiken took charge of her young life by launching her career and changing her name, complete with a last name she said she took from a former male lover. Mabley's early departure with the Theater Owners Booking Association (TOBA) circuit, or the so-called Chitlin Circuit, made it possible to use her body to make a living rather than to remain in Brevard and risk further sexual violations "and everything else," as she is quoted as saying in a brief reference to those violations.[4]

Black vaudeville performers were criticized for either upholding stereotypes from minstrel, blackface days that the emerging educated Black middle class was trying to avoid or they were celebrated for their creative genius. As Black vaudeville entertainers became more present by the beginning of the twentieth century, some avoided minstrelsy and others focused on musical comedy. The style and quality depended on the particular circuit and the audience. Shows would change to accommodate the move of Blacks from the rural southern cities to urban northern cities. For example, the Keith Circuit, which was managed by White men and primarily featured White acts, became known for presenting "clean" "coon acts."[5] Karen Sotiropoulos asserts, "In part, black performers saw opportunity on the vaudeville stage because the venue itself challenged traditional lines of respectability, offering newer, sanitized theatrical spaces suitable for middle-class as well as working-class audiences."[6] Free from the past they left behind, performers like Mabley could explore pleasures.

Despite the horrors of her childhood, Mabley was likely exposed to storytelling as part of her southern upbringing. When Mabley met the husband and wife comedy team known as Butterbeans and Susie in Houston, Texas, they were a successful and well-respected duo among their peers. Butterbeans was born Jodie Edwards in Georgia in 1895. At the age of twelve, he began his lifelong career as an entertainer when he worked as a dancer and performer with carnivals. Traveling on the circuit brought him in contact with Susie Hawthorne, who was born in Pensacola, Florida, in the late 1890s. Their act began in the Douglass Theatre in Macon, Georgia. Butterbeans, who named himself for the vaudeville performer Butler "String Beans" May, danced and Susie sang the blues. Feeling the synergy of their act, the two staged a public wedding as part of a paid publicity stunt at Philadelphia's Standard Theatre in May 1917. This marriage, which lasted until Susie's death in 1963, added a humorous contrived conflict to their act as a warring husband and wife. Their tour was popular during the 1920s and 1930s, leading them to begin recording their routines in 1924.[7] When the Great Depression hampered productivity in the recording industry, they remained relevant on the stage.

Butterbeans and Susie's routine joined elements of the blues with dancing and comedy. Surviving records show that, at times, Susie would berate Butterbeans for his infidelity and other times she would insist on him meeting her sexual needs. Regardless of the topic, they would always show their willingness to use double entendre to broach the subject of sex. Doing so kept them in business and out of jail. During this time, "The sense of shock at the mere mention of sex, together with the belief that those who flouted conventional standards of sexual morality or used sex for commercial gain were degenerates and perverts, were essential to the law's efforts to repress sexual freedom during the 1920s and 1930s."[8] This would change to some extent during Mabley's lifetime as she learned how to tease the forbidden without actually saying it. Surely, the rhetorical techniques aroused the naughty imaginative sensibilities of the couple's audience.

Their duets didn't silence one voice or favor another. As players, their banter shows them interacting equally with one another, even if one is more dominant than the other. Recording forced the stage performers to rely on dialogue and their vocal tones as opposed to facial expressions, hand gestures, and other body language used to convey the performance to their listening audience. As a result, the audience members must listen carefully for clues and use their imagination and interpretation to get enjoyment from the actors' recording.

Duet singing placed the two in a position of vying for power; they were often either in opposition to one another or in sync with one another. Barbara Monroe sees the connection between the blues and comedy. Of the common man and woman duos that were a popular act in vaudeville, she observes, "Both male and female singers celebrated the sexual enterprise, sometimes seen as a cooperative effort, but more often as a competitive one."[9] "Oh Yeah"[10] is an example of the power play among the two. Susie is the lead through her decision to leave Butterbeans, and he is in the position of begging her to stay with the response of "Oh No." Their movement from her "Oh Yeah" to his "Oh No" shows their command of wit to make their audience laugh. Like a blues song, the duet features a singer who is "a fool" for trusting the lover. Susie shares her vulnerability with Butterbeans, "Your actions have me lonely" for his sexual attention. With a serious tone, she humorously tells him, "I forgot the night you give me a small portion." In response, Butterbeans "swears" he will never mistreat her again, but Susie remains committed to her decisions. If Butterbeans will not meet her sexual needs in favor of an attraction to another, then she will not remain in a relationship with him. In "Hot Dog Man," she again takes the lead in expressing her desires for a man that can sexually meet her needs. Butterbeans may or may not be that man. Susie tells him she wants "a hot dog for my roll." Not only does she tell him what she wants, she tells him she wants a size that will "satisfy me." As an extension to "Hot Dog Man," in "Jelly Roll," she openly brags about her sexual ability. She proudly proclaims, "Ain't nobody in this town got no jelly roll like mine." Ignoring respectability and the women in the church, she tells him she is only interested in her physical experience. An emotional attachment is not wanted: "Don't want nobody to fall in love with me about this jelly roll." In contrast, their competition is analogous to playing the dozens, where "Elevator Papa, Switchboard Mama," finds Butterbeans and Susie playing a dueling pair. Both complain about a lack of sexual satisfaction. Susie's ability to draw attention to her own desires and sexual pleasures places her in a position of power as she uses her voice to publicly exercise her agency over her body. Simultaneously, she consistently rejects making Butterbeans feel as though he has control over her. If he does not do what she expects him to do, she will simply get rid of him and let him know why.

s: Lookie here, Mister Indoor Chauffeur.

B: What's wrong now?

s: Why, you ain't nothing but a low down loafer.

B: Stop that.

s: When I get in your car you keep getting so cold, believe me
   Butter someday I'm gonna get you told.

B: Now lookie here!

s: What is it?

B: Miss Switchboard Operator, I done found out that you ain't
   nothing but a real man hater, why in the world don't you tend to
   your own phone.

s: What do you mean?

B: And let a hardworking man alone.

s: Then listen, elevator papa, elevator papa.

B: Yes?

s: Seems like you always wanna go down.

B: Now lookie here.[11]

Neither one will admit to fault or apologize. This humorous back and forth is an expression of wants that will never be fulfilled, something a Black audience would know about, especially in the 1920s, and that fans of blues singers like Memphis Minnie would come to enjoy in the next decade. Although they were married, Butterbeans and Susie blatantly defied respectability in their performances. As the emerging Black middle class became more educated and tried to advance the race through education and other means, they would criticize any acts that relied on stereotypes as a form of entertainment. The duo crossed class lines and defied Black middle-class expectations with the purpose of making their audience laugh and have the experience of enjoyment; this was especially necessary for the working-class Blacks who saw them in the tent shows or in Black theaters. To be sure, "Butterbeans and Susie—and Tim Moore, Pigmeat Markham, Spider Bruce Mason and Dusty Fletcher, who followed them—did not set out to present an accurate portrayal of black people any more than Laurel or Hardy or The Three Stooges intended to represent white people. The point was to be funny . . ."[12] Despite criticism by those who did not approve of their sexually tinged comedy, the pair played with other blues singers who did not shy away from sexual performances, such as Ma Rainey. Susie performed with Bessie Smith and performed in the Cotton Club. They also appeared at the Apollo Theater.[13] There was clearly an interest among White audiences who had enjoyed being entertained by Negroes but also Black audiences who may have simply wanted to laugh and to escape the problems of Black life. As they flaunted their indulgence of pleasure, they teased their audience's need for pleasure.

Mabley would learn from Butterbeans and Susie that comics had a great deal of control over their art and that there would always be people willing to pay for the pleasure of laughter. For as long as she performed, from the interwar era through the civil rights movement, Black people needed to escape reality or at least laugh at the reality of their situation. Though Black performers certainly had to keep their audience's preferences in mind, they could also train their audiences by testing traditional boundaries. Mabley's use of the voice to entertain and to tell truth as a mother figure, inspired by her grandmother, was unusually empowering for a Black woman of her era. Unlike the Black women activists of the era who spoke to specific audiences on specific topics and unlike actresses who were more often given lines rather than writing them, Black comics could cover several topics in just a few minutes that were written by the comics themselves.

Susie and Mabley were part of a tradition of liars, as Zora Neale Hurston would call Black comedians, who told "tall tales" or stories to explain a situation. Within rural Black southern communities, women's play on comedy was not unusual. From blues singers who sang about beating their men to Black women, like Susie playing to her partner, Butterbeans, these were familiar interplays that had carried on for generations. Realizing this, Hurston captured the style of comedic women and the significance of their voices when they resisted submission from men. One of the most recognized occurs in *Their Eyes Were Watching God* (1937) when Janie tells her abusive husband Joe Clark, "When you pull down yo' britches, you look lak de change uh life."[14] Janie declares this in response to the man who requires her to wear her long hair wrapped because he has seen a man touching it without her knowledge, and after a number of physical and verbal abuses that cause her to recognize that "the spirit of the marriage had left."[15] Janie's strategic move from silence in the house to a public verbal assault on his sexual virility, or rather lack thereof, exposes his vulnerability to his male admirers. Unlike Susie, Janie uses her voice to disrupt a space rather than to bring joy to it. However, her voice brings her satisfaction that she has power that her husband fears she may use one day—and does. Where she had been told not to be involved with the comical banter, as it was designated unladylike behavior for her, she upsets the power of the space by daring to reclaim her voice in public—a voice her husband slowly but strategically took away in favor of his own. Hurston based the novel on her observant experiences: "As early as I could remember it was the habit of evenings to swap stories. Even the women folks would stop and break a breath with them at times. As a child when I was sent to Joe Clarke's store, I'd drag out my leaving as long as possible in order to hear more."[16] By consistently focusing on the lack of attraction to an old man, Moms Mabley would do something very similar in her act by using her childhood for inspiration.

Although Hurston was drawing from her childhood in all-Black Eatonville, a city she would reimagine in her work repeatedly during her career, she would be labeled as using a "minstrel technique that makes 'white folks' laugh."[17] In his review of *Their Eyes Were Watching God*, Richard Wright heavily criticized Hurston, "Her characters eat and laugh and cry and work and kill; they swing like a pendulum eternally in that safe and narrow orbit in which America likes to see the Negro live; between laughter and tears."[18] Wright derisively criticized a Black woman who dared to find moments of pleasure in southern living as inauthentic. In his article, "Why Richard Wright Hated Zora Neale Hurston," Henry Louis Gates Jr. surmises that Wright was writing against, "Hurston's creation of a black female protagonist who was comfortable with and celebrated her own sensuality, and who insisted on her right to choose her own lovers in spite of the strictures of the black community."[19] In sum, Hurston was being criticized for allowing a Black woman to search for and find her own form of pleasure.

Hurston saw pleasure in sex and love, but in comedy and social interaction as well. *Mules and Men* expands her work on the study of storytelling and comedy for Black people to Black people. Of her storytelling collections, Sharon L. Jones asserts, "Her folklore expeditions also reveal the politics of race, class, and cultures."[20] Hurston admits to seeing that the lies serve more than a "theory" of telling stories that act as a form of "resistance" cloaked under "a lot of laughter and pleasantries,"[21] for Black people, especially when White audiences were present: "The white man is always trying to know into somebody else's business. All right, I'll set something outside the door of my mind for him to play with and handle. He can read my writing but he sho' can't read my mind. I'll put this play toy in his hand, and he will seize it and go away. Then I'll say my say and sing my song."[22]

Hurston, whose collection of stories she recorded, transcribed, and published as *Mules and Men*, funded by Charlotte Osgood Mason and read by Franz Boas, two White people, makes a statement of resistance by acknowledging that she is aware of the censoring powers of White patrons. Yet, the Black artist still holds the power of their voice and art. Telling lies is one such way in which this technique is enacted.

Despite the need to walk very fine social and political lines, something African Americans had been doing since slavery, Black theater and performance continued to grow in popularity as it moved from the all-Black audiences of the vaudeville circuit to the mainstream. Audiences were always important and Hurston knew this when she placed Janie on the forbidden stage. Interested in bringing more attention to the play between women and men and how women were empowered by this play, she traveled the South and gathered stories.

As the storyteller, Hurston's *Mules and Men* is layered with stories told by women and men and about women and men. Her power of voice and pen is unyielding. As a fiction writer, she built scenes that interweave introductions to stories and that begin or end with a contextual interplay often involving a man trying to interfere with the woman's telling of a story. Whose story is better? Or more accurate? This is hilarious as they are all lying. The power lies in the ability to tell the story or to take the stage and draw the audience's attention. Hurston's retelling of a story by a woman named Shug is an example of this. At one point, Shug can only do this when Bennie, who demands to tell his story about "womens" chasing men, loses his battle for consciousness to the potency of their homemade liquor. Bennie tells his stepsister, "Ah don't want to lissen to no ole talk 'bout three mens after no one 'oman. It's always more'sn three womens after every man." Refuting what he knows by asserting what she knows, Shug counters, "Well, de way Ah know de story, there was three mens after de same girl."[23] Bennie falls asleep and is silenced, perhaps by the woman who ultimately controls the master narrative. Hurston begins the next chapter with Shug telling the story of what happened when "three mens went to court a girl." In her story, the father and his daughter "couldn't decide" so the father tells the men to return in the morning and have a contest. The one "dat can do de quickest trick kin have de girl."[24] One man was commended for fixing a bucket to hold water as he carried it for ten miles. A second suitor impressed with his remarkable ability to cut down ten acres of wood, plough the field, plant peas, and grow them in time for dinner. The third won when he shot a gun and ran back in time to place a deer in front of the bullet. In sum, Shug resists the narrative that Bennie proposes by telling a story that is analogous to a stand-up act where she mocks men's bravado or claims of extraordinary physical abilities through the performance of "tricks."

Highly influenced by Black southern women like those Hurston described, her grandmother, and Susie, Mabley learned to hone her comedic skills as a stand-up comedienne. In addition, her younger brother "Eddie Patton wrote situations for her, but most of her material was absorbed from listening to her world."[25] Rather than to tell lies, or admit to telling them, Mabley told the "truth" to her audience. As Black people began to move from the South to the North and women began to move into male-dominated spaces in urban areas that were left vacant because of World War I, Moms Mabley emigrated from the South through the Black vaudeville circuit and transitioned into performing in respected Black theaters in cities such as Washington, DC, and Harlem, New York. Entering the professional entertainment industry at the time of the Harlem Renaissance, Mabley represented a figure of transition that bridged Black southern comedic musical traditions with White northern curiosities. Mabley relied on storytelling to appeal to the audience's imagination. Storytelling gives the listener an opportunity to travel to places unknown and to see the impossible happen. It is empowering for both the teller and the listener. Further, it gives the teller pleasure in being the center of attention. When the teller is speaking, she can manipulate the listener into believing in the possibility that some part of the story is true. As the best pleasurable experience, a story holds attraction. There is teasing, an introduction, a climax, and a conclusion. If the teller is successful, she leaves the listener wanting more.

When Mabley began building her career in New York in the 1920s, she was among the growing class of African American and Caribbean immigrants who were moving to Harlem in search for better opportunities. Lynching in the South, segregationist practices in the Caribbean and the South, and job opportunities in northern cities (as opposed to field work) made New York and other cities, such as Chicago and Detroit, attractive. Although Black folks would soon learn that there was no escaping racism, living among each other in Harlem made moving worth the risk. They would also still find themselves working in low-paying jobs and paying high rents, leading to rent parties as another way to address needs and to escape the reality of the need. It was at these events that Langston Hughes recalled that "the dancing and singing and impromptu entertaining went on until dawn came in at the windows."[26] Problems may very well have formed communities that celebrated their hard-earned accomplishments. James F. Wilson concurs, "In black publications such as the *Amsterdam News*, *New York Age*, *Inter-State Tattler*, and the *Messenger*, black journalists and essayists triumphantly declared the political, academic, and cultural accomplishments of Harlem residents even more boldly than they did the terrifying housing statistics, arrests, and artistic disappointments."[27] Harlem highlighted the pleasure of advancement as a means to overcome the problems.

Harlem began to become the capital of Black entertainment. Blues and jazz clubs opened to accommodate growing tastes for Black entertainment. One of the most popular was the Cotton Club, which, as Lena Horne describes, hired Black entertainers for the enjoyment of White patrons. Lincoln and Crescent Theatres began presenting Black entertainment to Black audiences in 1914. Mabley crossed some of the boundaries when she "began entertaining at night clubs, such as the Cotton Club, Connie's Inn, and the Savoy Ballroom."[28] In the Cotton Club, which only catered to White audiences who could afford a high cover charge, she opened for the most revered jazz performers of their day, including "Duke Ellington, Louis Armstrong, Bennie Goodman, Count Basie, and the late Cab Calloway."[29] On the other hand, Black theaters and clubs provided work for Black entertainers and pleasure for Black audiences who were not welcomed elsewhere. Mabley performed in many such segregated spaces early in her career. Williams observes, "The black theaters provided a place for the entertainers and audiences alike 'to be somebody,' for the entertainers to perfect their craft and for the audiences to hear their music, see their own dances, and relax in congenial laughter."[30] Dealing with the restrictions on Black entertainers, she was forced but poised to play different roles. In 1923, she played a minor role in Henri Bowman's *Cotton Blossom*, a product of the TOBA circuit that ran at the Lincoln Theatre in New York. She also played with Zora Neale Hurston in *Fast and Furious: A Colored*

Revue in 1931, which opened on September 15 and closed a week later because of bad reviews. The women collaborated in writing some of the scenes and acting in a skit. According to Hurston's biographer, Robert Hemenway, Hurston wrote "three sketches, and made her dramatic debut as a pompom girl in a sketch about a football game; her sister cheerleader was a pre-'Moms' Jackie Mabley."[31] We can only imagine how much the two learned from one another and how this collaboration influenced their future work. In 1932, Mabley had a role in a Broadway musical revue, *Blackberries*, and seven years later she performed in *Swingin' the Dreams*, "a jazz adaptation of Shakespeare's *A Midsummer Night's Dream*."[32] Mabley was persistent in trying new opportunities to gain prominence as a performer. A year later, in 1933, she had a brief appearance with Paul Robeson in *The Emperor Jones*. A role that differed significantly from the Moms persona, Mabley as Marcella is introduced to the tall handsome Brutus Jones (played by Robeson), shakes his hand and flirts with him by batting her eyelashes and touching her upper chest. Marcella, the manager of the "house," or cabaret, is wearing a skirt suit with a white shirt, distinguishing her from the other dainty women who are wearing form-fitting dresses. Marcella roughly handles a patron who gets out of hand by grabbing ahold of him and ushering him out of the room. Mabley had entered a fickle industry. It would be nearly forty years before she had another film role and stage performances were inconsistent. Reportedly, "Hughes wrote a friend that he occasionally helped Mabley financially."[33]

The Apollo Theater of Harlem would be the place where she found regular work when she became the first comedienne to appear there in 1940. The gig lasted fifteen weeks. After some years of operating as a burlesque theater, it opened in 1934 under the ownership of Sidney Cohen and was managed by Morris Sussman. Its opening show was Jazz a la Carte, headlined by Benny Carter and His Orchestra.[34] The Apollo continued to hold its importance according to Lonnie Bunch, fourteenth secretary of the Smithsonian Institute, who came to appreciate its importance based on his observations of the men in his family. In commemoration of the theater's seventy-fifth anniversary, Bunch recalls the shows elicited, "joy, enthusiasm, and laughter" or a time of much-needed pleasure to deal with "the ways of white folks in North Carolina, the women who broke their hearts, or whether life was harder working for the railroad or toiling in the factories in Newark, New Jersey.[35] From the men, he would learn why the stage was so inviting:

> One after another, these old men talked about how they were moved by the music that emanated from the Apollo, be it Duke Ellington, Lionel Hampton, Billie Holiday, or Newark's own Sarah Vaughn. They laughed as they shared lines that they had heard from the routines of Moms Mabley, Timmie Rogers, or Pigmeat Markham, lines that were exciting and risqué to a teenager on the verge of adulthood. These comic riffs allowed them to find relief from the realities of race, even if it lasted only as long as the joke being told. Since I never heard of any of these people, I asked just what is the Apollo? Someone answered, "It is a place where we got to be who we are and maybe who we want to be."[36]

In other words, the Apollo stage was a site for hope and relief from the reality of the problems that Black Americans faced. It was not a place where social problems were solved, but it was a place that allowed Black folks to see themselves in a Black comedian's scenario or to hear themselves in a Black singer's or musician's song. Significantly, Black comedians' jokes gave them power to influence the mood of the listener and to call out a situation that was unfair. To be sure, it was a center for Black joy where pleasures could be shared by the community.

It was also a place where the stage operated as a center of empowerment. Bunch's memory reveals how their discussions brought their family together. Just mentioning the Apollo could make a family laugh, talk, and enjoy a pleasurable memory. Each person listening to a comedian may hear or feel something different than another because a statement has appeal to the different experiences of the listener. Bunch goes further, "the Apollo [is] a place of possibility: a place of possibility that reflected and mediated the tensions between aspiration and reality, between those who owned the means of production and accessibility and those who produced the culture, and between cultural innovation and the celebration of tradition."[37] What they share is the laughter, the moment of joy and of relief. Such an experience was affirmation of their humanity.

Mabley would become successful through her understanding of how to mediate the tensions Bunch describes. First, she created a persona that allowed her to access the stage. Barbara Monroe describes her as having a "wanton persona."[38] Although the first woman to appear at the Apollo, she would become known and respected among the men for her generosity and friendship, but also for her gambling skills. According to dancer Norma Miller, "Moms ruled the Apollo Theater. She was the dominant force."[39] When referenced among her peers, her name is the only woman's name that is cited, as Bunch shows, with Pigmeat Markham and Timmie Rogers. Mabley understood that her presence as a Black woman in an industry that was dominated by men was not going to be welcomed. During the interwar era, Black women were challenged with being taken seriously as actresses, dancers, and singers. As noted by Lena Horne, skin color mattered even to those Blacks who hired Black women for roles on the stage. With a preference for light skin in America's most revered places of entertainment, brown-toned Mabley was strategic in appearing as a woman who was not trying to entice men with her looks. She presented just the opposite: a woman wearing moderate makeup, a bonnet, socks, flat shoes, and a house dress. In her later years, she presented without her teeth. According to H. Alexander Welcome, "Mabley's stage persona, Moms, was based on Mabley's own grandmother. An elderly woman attempting to teach her children . . ."[40] More specifically, Williams notes that the persona developed in the "twenties onward."[41] Though Mabley did not present as a mammy figure, she also was not relegated to a jezebel or a sexy seductress. She refused to present herself as a domestic on stage, although she did perform as a maid for a Black family later in her career.[42] In his study of her defiance, Terrance Tucker observes, "Mabley's move away from casting herself in the domestic space, in her real life as well as her humor, contrasts with stereotypical notions of African American female work and traditional female subject matter."[43] Instead, her homely appearance was complemented by jokes that skirt the line of sex. Indeed, her persona could be unexpectedly enigmatic to new audiences. Moms's persona successfully worked within an Apollo that catered to a "respectable middle-class."[44]

Secondly, she created an act that allowed her to lightly but purposefully navigate political restrictions. New York may have been the place for performers to make a living, but there were many restrictions that suppressed and repressed the public indulgence of pleasures. The hope of the nation to be moral and pure came through the prohibition of alcohol in the 1920s. Legal action would be taken against anyone who violated restrictions on speech, including making explicit references to sex or appearing nude.

Moving from subject to subject, Mabley's stories were short and to the point, bringing her audience an experience inspired by her contrived confusion, joy, and pleasure. Tucker asserts further that Mabley, "Immersed in African American folk humor . . . adopted its tradition of moving from subversion to reversal to confrontation."[45] In a 1948 performance, perhaps the earliest existing recording of her work, "Don't Sit on My Bed,"[46] she guides her audience from one inappropriate comment to the other. And in all her scenarios, she is in charge as she begins with telling her audience the truth that Mother Hubbard would not tell. According to her, Mother Hubbard went to the cupboard to get a cup of gin. Here she retells the story of the Mother Goose rhyme from a different perspective. From the beginning of the routine, then, she lets the audience know that she may look like a mother who is wearing a simple dress and hat, but she does not fit the traditional perspective that the audience may have of a mother and certainly not that of a Black mother. She is neither meek nor quiet as expressed through the gruffness of her voice. She shouts to the audience, "you in the back need to laugh a little louder so I can hear you." She commands them to participate through her call and response, and they oblige her. This calling to the audience for their attention transitions her into a story where she tells them how she ended up "dropping her drawers" on a plane. But she does not linger long on the visual, which she suggests was a misunderstanding, a moment of innocence enacted by a woman who did not understand what the flight attendant was saying to her to alleviate her ear problems, but we must remember that she has told us that she was on her way to the White House by invitation. Eventually Mabley was invited to White House by Presidents John F. Kennedy and Lyndon Johnson.[47]

Mabley had a way of manipulating spaces in which she did not belong by insisting that she did belong. This happens through multidimensional perspectives. When Black comedians crossed over from a Black audience to a White one, they had to make comedy universal. To achieve this, Mabley chose to place herself in places where Black people would not have been associated. More specifically, audiences are forced not just to see her on the stage performing for their enjoyment but they must simultaneously travel with her on a plane. How many Black folks would a White audience have seen on any plane? They must also envision her in the White House, not as a maid but as an invited guest. Consequently, the audience must suspend any limited beliefs they have of a Black woman, a woman that they may not have paid much attention to under any other circumstances, and see her. She impresses upon them various levels of discomfort as she moves spatially from one restricted space to another.

After moving from public spaces, she takes them to a private space in her house. Moms Mabley shifts from a comical stance to a more serious one as she sings a song about her house rules. As her guest, a person has a variety of choices of where to sit, but *do not* sit on her bed. By placing boundaries in her home, she resists any attempts at familiarity that calling her Moms may lead someone to think he/she/they can exercise with her. By subverting the making of boundaries from the restrictor to the restricted, Williams notes, "In addition to bonding with her audience, assuming the maternal pose provided Mabley with a vehicle for boundary setting—for controlling the relationship between herself (the performer) and the audience."[48] As an intimate space, she also, as a woman who knows violation, is clear to express agency over her body. Mabley's dominance of the stage is an exercise of her position to be both heard and seen. Ultimately, she used comedy to command respect that would extend outside the comedy stage.

During her long career, Mabley covered a variety of topics. I will focus on her style of truth-telling to impress upon her growing audience the need for social progress. These particular topics are featured on the *Best of Moms Mabley and Pigmeat* album released in 1964. By the time of the civil rights movement, Moms was still continuing to perform, but her popularity gained new audiences when she recorded her live performances. Recording allowed her to cross racial barriers from the all-Black audiences of the vaudeville and interwar days to attract the attention of White men who had platforms for comedians who could appeal to their audiences. Tucker observes that Mabley maintained a "symbiotic relationship between performer and audience."[49] Mabley's album rarely points to race, but neither did she in the feature described above in 1948. In fact, some of her truth-telling in "Don't Sit on My Bed" can be found on the album. To be sure, her performances proved to be translatable across race, class, and time.

In her joke about a man's hairstyle, she uses him to make a point about the importance of not resisting progress.

Hey Son, Come here a minute. Mom gotta little secret to tell you though. Mom want you to get along and be a great boy in the world. You know and Mom is very interested in young men. You tall enough. You young enough. But they don't wear that kind of hair anymore. (pause for three seconds to loud laughter from audience)
What kind of hair grease is that you wearing?
Man responds. (inaudible)
Oh, Madame Walker. Well tell Madame to walk around them edges a little bit better. (loud laughter from the audience)[50]

A Black audience would have understood the punchline of this joke without any need for explanations or asides. Monroe finds that "Ritualistic insult structured her routines."[51] First, since she was known for her attraction to young men, she lures him and the audience in by showing interest in his age and his height. Then she takes an unexpected turn to tell him the "truth" about his hair. By casting the gaze on his hair, she uses the style as a metaphor for social progress. Several of the jokes on this particular album are about time and the need for change. Styles change and she signals to the man that she may be old, but as he matures, he (substitute any man) must change his attitude as well. Moms uses the stage to resist an unwillingness to indulge the pleasures that come with social progress by making change attractive. For men who have ways that tend to restrict women, she is speaking against this. In another joke on the track, she makes this clear.

Moms mastered the technique of truth-telling. In the track titled "Nursery Rhymes" she uses a significantly different voice— one that makes her sound like a woman of advanced age—to present herself as the truth-telling Mother Goose. In this act, as she did in "Don't Sit on My Bed," she presents a counter-discourse to Mother Goose rhymes, but she gives more attention to the rhymes. What is most important is her introduction of why telling the truth is important. Truth functions as a form of education and education leads to a progressive society.

Moms wrote her Mother Goose book and I want you to buy it. And if you don't want your children to know the truth about . . . I'm gonna tell them the truth, hear?

You tell them Mother Hubbard gave the dog a bone. I say Mother Hubbard has her gin in the cupboard.

You tell them Jack and Jill went up the hill after some water. I tell them water don't run up hill.

You tell them the wolf ate up Red Riding Hood's grandmother. I tell them if he did he must have used tenderizer on her as tough as grandma was.[52]

Although not all of these references are from Mother Goose rhymes, her point is to make people laugh while subverting the stories to tell it from her perspective. Moms, in opposition to the ideal of the Mother Goose figure, has already established that she learned about telling the truth from her centurion-aged southern grandmother. Her truth is from the perspective of an elderly Black mother who feels responsible for young listeners of the new age. If Mother Goose rhymes and children's stories such as "Little Red Riding Hood" are meant to entertain and to tell a thematic tale of how to use wit and wisdom to overcome adversity or danger, Moms's "truths" will do the same. Two of these revisions focus on women's actions. Mother Hubbard does not go to the cupboard to feed her dog; she goes to the cupboard to find something that will bring her pleasure: a cup of gin. Grandmother was not simply killed by the wolf, but she fought for her life rather than submit to the inevitable. Moms's grandmother was not a meek little old vulnerable lady as depicted in the story books.

Mabley's revision is most certainly as racial as it is gendered. She is fully aware of the stories as being marketed toward White children. The popularity of these rhymes and stories were published in books with illustrations of White children and a White mother. Moms's Jack and Jill will not be going in the wrong direction to find what they need to sustain their lives. As she opens this act, she tells her civil rights audience that she is speaking about change:

Getting back to my book. (laughter) I had wrote a book for my teenagers. Ya'll call 'em delinquents and everything else, but I love 'em. They buy Moms records. They love Mom. They dig Mom. And Mom dig them.

You don't dig 'em because you way back in hither time and you ain't gon change and that's what's wrong with the country now, especially America, you've got to change with the times. . . . Like a lot of old men say, (change voice and tone to project performance of an old man) "Well times ain't like they used to be." I said, "I'm glad of it." Who want times like they used to be?

Notably, the change that she speaks of is directed from the audience to old men. Seeing old men as the keepers of practices that she personally has experienced as harmful, she revises the rhymes to disrupt the practice of passing down prejudiced ideas from one generation to another.

In fact, one of her favorite subjects was to talk about her disdain of old men and her attraction to young men. In her stand-up, an area of entertainment dominated by men, her presence gave her a sense of power. If a man could make jokes about women, then Mabley countered their jokes with hers about her preference for young men. Tucker observes, "Her expressions of desire for young men signified on historical male desire for younger women to reinvigorate them or to resolve their midlife crises."[53] He goes on, "Playing on the assumptions embedded in the more acceptable pairing of older men and younger women, Mabley challenged the role of the passive female object that was often part of male comic routines."[54] Mabley developed her signature act about her dislike for old men over her career. Presenting "Mom's Old Man" as physically fragile and relatively useless elicited laughter from multiple audiences who all had some understanding of aging and the toll it takes on a body. Ironically, as Mabley got older, her dislike of old men and her jokes about them continued to resonate as Moms most certainly did not want a man older than she to care for.

These jokes had the effect of speaking to her desire for experiences that were not burdensome but that allowed her to indulge her own joy. In *Moms Mabley: Live at Sing Sing*, [55] released in 1967, she starts by definitively and unashamedly telling Moms's truth with a tone of disgust, "I don't like no old men. (laughter and applause) I don't want nothing old but some old money. And I am going to use it to put an ad in the paper for some young man." After a few more derisions, she goes on, "An old man don't know how to do nothing." In her portrayal of an elderly man's voice, she says he asked her to sit down to talk. She set him down first (laughter) "and then I set down." In this bit, Moms relays the limits and restrictions associated with older men. His needs come first and she is uninterested in putting herself second to a man who "don't know how to do nothing but be old." By sharing her blatant dislike of old men, she resists the kind of control that he represents where such a relationship would promise to get worse and never improve, until he is gone. To that, she expressed relief: "I am so glad my Old Man is dead."

Not only does the old man represent a lack of social progress and personal control but he also represents suppression of desire. There is a double entendre in her assertion that "an old man don't know how to do nothing." She makes it clear that she receives no enjoyment from the man, who is physically unattractive and, we can safely presume, unable to satisfy her sexually. His fragile body makes touch impossible as he is so weak that "a leaf fell on him and knocked him out." Knowing her biography, this may also be a way of expressing her resistance toward the rapes that occurred when she was a child by older men. L. H. Stallings surmises, "what remains clear is that century after century Black women's discussions about sexuality in critical and creative efforts, as well as real life and fiction, have been marred by the notion of silence, secrecy, and whispers. Some Black women may have been longing to tell, but there were those Black women who have been telling, and in the telling they have been bawdy, explicit, and downright shameless in their expressions of sexual desires, despite reprimands they may have received. It is those voices that we still have trouble celebrating."[56] To be sure, her amplified voice and position on the stage gave her the power to resist and to involve masses of people in resistance, even if they are not fully aware of the role they play as participants. Mabley through Moms is in control.

When Moms Mabley appeared at the Playboy Club with Sammy Davis Jr. in 1970, Davis, a well-known Black actor, comedian, and dancer who had crossed racial boundaries, told the audience that Moms's name was given to her because of her generosity among younger people in the industry. The name allowed her "to claim her community and the world as her family and craftily orchestrate a comedic performance stitched together from the cultural shreds of African American people."[57] Though not much is known about her personal life, by all accounts, Mabley was a complex, proud woman who lived separately from the persona she presented on stage. She is known to have been a frequent visitor at Harlem's Abyssinian Church where she attended Sunday services. As a Christian woman who was dedicated to her family and who loved women, she mediated the stage and her personal life in such a way that each decade drew her closer to financial stability and career success.

Although Moms was only interested in young men, Mabley was interested in young women. Brittney Cooper provides context, "The regime of respectability, which called into being a culture of dissemblance, proceeded upon the fundamental belief that it was detrimental for Black women to actively signal a sexual or erotic self in public, because such significations would make them vulnerable to rape."[58] Mabley controlled the audience's gaze by spotlighting Moms's heterosexual desire. However, in her private life, her same-sex relationships were not a secret. Norma Miller, who shared a dressing room with her at the Apollo, also says she shared it with Mabley's lover. She reveals further, "We never called her gay. We called her Mr. Mom." When she was offstage, she replaced the Moms costume with "tailored slacks, silk blouses . . . shoes" and on Sundays she wore hats. When she traveled, she wore men's attire and she would present herself in this attire in signed photos that she shared with others. She is also known to have been "an avid reader and an attractive woman who wore furs, chic clothes, and owned a Rolls-Royce, albeit an iterate smoker, a card shark, and a whiz at checkers."[59] Mabley carefully skirted respectability by keeping her sexual identity out of the spotlight and away from her voyeurs; on the stage her act pushed boundaries. In other words, she consistently resisted repression of who she was as a woman.

Her truth was considered illegal. Same-sex relationships were labeled sinful and perverse. William E. Nelson notes, "The New York judiciary likewise showed no interest in giving homosexuals freedom to pursue their sexual practices. Until the 1940s, judges routinely defended conventional Victorian morality for the twin purposes of preventing 'disorder and anarchy' and protecting 'our women and children.'"[60] More recent scholarship has looked at the subcultures of the Harlem Renaissance, that is the private spaces that were created as a safe-place for Black people who were interested in indulging their same-sex desires. Mabley had been known to attend the risqué parties of A'Lelia Walker, whose mother, Madame C. J. Walker, became wealthy from the sales of her hair products. In contrast to the Black working-class rent parties, Walker's parties catered to the famous and wealthy. Private parties, such as those hosted by Walker, were "notorious for their sexual experimentation" and provided "private parties in Harlem . . . protected spaces for lesbians, bisexuals, and gay men to meet and mingle."[61] Not surprisingly, among her featured guests of Black entertainers "ranging from famous jazz and blues performers" was Jackie "Moms" Mabley. The comedienne was also rumored to have been the lover of Odesa Madre, who was known as the "Queen of black Washington." Madre, who owned "nightclubs, brothels, and gambling rings" was as open about her preference for women lovers as she was about flaunting her wealth.[62] Of Madre, George Yancy notes that, "Not only did Madre exercise Black *womanist* self-determination in a world of white racism, but she also resisted confinement within a male-dominated and restrictive space of domesticity."[63] Mabley and Madre were well matched in this sense. They may have met before Mabley moved to New York, during the time she lived in Washington, DC, where she "purchased a family home at First and R Streets, Northwest" for her mother to live in before she was killed in an accident in 1946.[64]

In keeping with the changing society, she would eventually feel comfortable broaching homosexuality with her audience. During her *Live at Sing Sing* performance, she tells a series of anecdotes to show how bad things are "out there" to illustrate to the audience why she felt warmer and safer with them. At one point, she tells the audience of inmates that a bar owner was without a bartender and had to hire a "sissy boy." There is a moment of low grumbling and laughter. She pauses, laughs, and scolds them, "Now don't you all make like you don't know what I'm talking about." With this guidance, she brings the audience members to where she is and releases them from any discomfort they may feel. They respond with loud laughter. She goes on, after the owner threatens to beat the "boy" if he steals anything else, she hits the punchline, "Alright, now kiss me and go to work." The audience erupts in laughter.

Moms remained busy until her death and she understood by 1974 how she could leverage her Moms persona to gain new audiences. She starred in *Amazing Grace*, a film about a widow who takes on corrupt politicians in Baltimore, and she does an adept job touching on the issues that the film addresses. In an interview that occurred shortly after she had a heart attack filming *Amazing Grace* and a year before her death, to appeal to a wide audience, Moms embraced the American idea and condemned the "scandal," a reference to the Watergate investigation that would eventually lead to President Nixon's resignation. Embracing her nationality at the time the country was dealing with a national scandal, she proclaimed her own position, "I am an American. I am not from Africa. I am an American."

In this rare interview,[65] she was most certainly speaking as an actress who was intent on promoting the film. One reason she gives for people seeing the film is that, "It's a movie that you can take your children to see. If it wasn't I wouldn't be in it. I live my life on the stage like I do in the street. I wouldn't do anything on there that I wouldn't want my children to see . . . then they wouldn't love Moms." Of course, Moms Mabley the comedienne was well known for telling jokes that were not for children. And, Jackie Mabley's preference for women was not shared with her fans. One area where Jackie and Moms met may have been her Christian beliefs. When asked, "What do you want to say to the young people?" she said, "You have to watch as well as pray . . . Start 'em when they young to know who God is . . . There is a higher being . . . God put me in show business." Jackie "Moms" Mabley died in 1975 from a heart attack. If this interview is any indication of how she wanted to be remembered, Christianity was the prism by which she wanted her audience to see her and the career that she built.

Moms Mabley was a pioneering woman who daringly left an unsafe home environment when she was still a child. Through her persistence, she honed her craft as a comedienne and used her voice to critique the society that she lived in as a Black woman. From this work, she took immense pleasure in her ability to make people laugh and to encourage her growing and changing audiences to see Black people beyond the stereotypes. From her, we also learn what it meant to have a personal life that was not defined by the public in the changing twentieth century. As a queer Black woman she would eventually lead her audience in seeing LGBTQ individuals in America through her art. Jackie "Moms" Mabley was an artist who succeeded in writing her own narrative of pleasure.

FIG. 1. Young Yolande Du Bois (Used with permission by the Department of Special Collections and University Archives, W.E.B. Du Bois Library, University of Massachusetts Amherst)

FIG. 2. Lena Horne as Georgia Brown with Eddie Anderson in *Cabin in the Sky* (Used with permission by Getty Images, Donaldson Collection)

FIG. 3. Lena Horne as Selina Rogers in *Stormy Weather* (Used with permission by Getty Images, George Rinhart)

FIG. 4. Memphis
Minnie circa
1928 (Used with
permission by Getty
Images, Donaldson
Collection)

FIG. 5. Memphis
Minnie and Kansas
Joe McCoy circa
1928 (Used with
permission by Getty
Images, Michael
Ochs Archives)

FIG. 6. Jackie "Moms" Mabley circa 1970 (Used with permission by Getty Images, Michael Ochs Archives)

FIG. 7. Jackie Mabley as "Moms" circa 1970 (Used with permission by Getty Images, Michael Ochs Archives)

4

Memphis Minnie and Songs
of Pleasure

As Jackie Mabley created Moms, Lizzie Douglas created the brash and sassy Memphis Minnie. Parsing out the complexity of a Memphis Minnie performance, Langston Hughes marvels at her body, her voice, and her presence at the dawn of a new year. Taking notice of her as an embodied dichotomy, Memphis Minnie's words are largely silenced under Hughes's observant gaze. He describes to his *Chicago Defender* audience: "She dresses neatly and sits straight in her chair perched on top of the refrigerator where the beer is kept."[1] A critic of respectability, Hughes attempted to unveil the contours of a woman whose dress and straight-back demeanor is complicated by her presence in a blues club. Hughes goes further to paint a colorful portrait of a vibrant Black woman at work, describing her "feet in her high-heeled shoes," "her thin legs," "her gold teeth," "dark red nails," and other details of her appearance. Is she a respectable lady or not? The revered writer's description of her appearance limits her to the point that readers never hear much of her voice or what she is singing to entertain her audience on New Year's Eve 1942, as World War II rages.

My intent in this chapter is to move beyond the gaze and to listen to the narrative cacophony of pleasure-seeking Black women's voices that Memphis Minnie conjured in her music during the interwar period of the 1930s. Memphis Minnie, who began recording in 1929, developed a performative persona that captured the attention of her male peers and made her a legend among them. Often overlooked by scholars in favor of earlier blues women, such as Gertrude "Ma" Rainey and Bessie Smith, Memphis Minnie was a major presence in the genre of southern country blues music who crossed her own gender and regional boundaries. Beginning with the 1920s, as Angela Davis has said of blues women pioneers, they "embodied sexualities associated with working-class black life—which, fatally, was seen by some [Harlem] Renaissance strategists as antithetical to the aims of their cultural movement—their music was designed as 'low' culture in contrast, for example, to endeavors such as sculpture, painting, literature, and classical music (through which the spirituals could be reformed)."[2] Davis's description perfectly fits themes resonating from Memphis Minnie, who became known as the "Queen of the Blues," and who not only gave voice to an individual self but also used the blues as a kind of news outlet to inform her listeners of the decisions women make for any number of reasons. Pleasure, for Memphis Minnie, was enacted in a myriad of ways such as crossing gender and racial boundaries, submitting to a lover, being controlling or resisting a lover, criticizing social inequality, or maybe a combination of these. Decisions she made in her personal life to build her career and to balance that career with romantic partners who were fellow musicians demonstrate her ability to seize pleasure as an artist, as much as her music shows her willingness to testify about how she proposed to enjoy who she was as a Black woman with sexual desires and the desire for gender and social equality in a segregated America.

Memphis Minnie, as her name suggests, was a woman of the South. On June 3, 1897, she was born Lizzie Douglas in Algiers, Louisiana, the first port where enslaved Africans were brought into the New Orleans area. According to her biographers, her parents, Abe Douglas and Gertrude Wells, were people of modest means who relied on sharecroppers' earnings to feed their growing family. Known as "Kid" by her family and later as Memphis Minnie by her fans, she was the oldest of thirteen children, but only nine survived into adulthood. At the age of seven, her parents left Algiers and moved to Walls, Mississippi, where they raised animals and sugarcane, cotton, and other crops.[3] Luckily for Minnie, who was not interested in farming, Walls is approximately twenty miles from Memphis.

If freedom of movement is a theme of blues music, Memphis Minnie would pursue it liberally at an early age. According to biographers Paul and Beth Garon, she was "a wild youngster who never took to the farming life and she ran away from home at an early age,"[4] hence the name "Kid" to capture her rambunctious spirit.[5] Not long after her parents moved to Walls, in 1905, she received a banjo from her father as a Christmas present, which led her to begin "playing for neighborhood parties."[6] Though it is not known what motivated her father to give her this gift, what is clear is that he provided his eldest daughter with a means to amplify her voice. And, he provided her with a ticket to free herself from Walls and pursue her musical interests. By the age of fifteen she boldly moved beyond the neighborhood parties and ran away to the corners of Memphis's Beale Street where she, as Kid Douglas, played a guitar she had purchased.[7] Eventually, she did as many aspiring Black performers, such as Ma Rainey and Bessie Smith before her, and joined touring shows where she developed her ability to captivate audiences under the most trying of circumstances. During World War II, she toured through Texas with Ringling Brothers.

No matter where she traveled, using "Memphis" as part of her name rooted her to the South and gave her music an identity. Memphis, Tennessee, is a southern town that dealt with violent racism. In 1892, anti-lynching activist Ida B. Wells had to leave Memphis when her office was destroyed by racists who, to say the least, were not pleased with her work. Providing historical context, Margaret McKee and Fred Chisenhall note: "The rampant racism and injustice, the fear and frustration, helped make Memphis a part of the northward migration that put thousands of southern blacks on the move. The outbreak of World War I and the resulting shortage of labor for northern factories had prompted efforts to lure blacks northward. Labor agents came to the South to recruit workers. The flow to the north was heightened by the 1915 floods and the onslaught of the boll weevil, which left planters in straightened circumstances, unable to employ as many workers as in the past."[8] Given that her family was in the agricultural industry, pursuing music was just as risky a career to pursue as any other for poor working-class Blacks, especially those who hoped to leave the South. Rather than to become trapped in a job that would let her survive, Kid Douglas decided to find one that would give her pleasure.

Spending time on Beale Street may have been dangerous, but it was a strategic move for the aspiring blues artist. It was the capitol of Black life in Memphis. Beale Street began to get attention when Robert Church, whose father was White, purchased property on the street left vacant by people who had not fared well during the 1878 yellow fever epidemic. One of the properties was Church's Park, an auditorium that seated 2,000 people and welcomed Black folks. By his death in 1912, Beale Street had also become the location of "theaters, vaudeville houses and moving picture shows."[9] One local described the emerging Beale Street as a "mile-long adventure" where "you could find surcease from sorrow; on Beale you could forget for a shining moment the burden of being black and celebrate being black; on Beale you could be a man, your own man; on Beale you could be free."[10] In sum, Beale Street was a center of Black pleasure. Like segregated Black communities, Beale Street was diverse. It was the location of bars that featured some of the best music in the Black South and it was the location of doctors' offices and other professional services. These services also included prostitution and illegal drug sales. It could be a violent place, a gangster's dream, especially at night, but it was also the place where people with musical talents tried to live out their dreams.

Beale Street was where a life could begin and another could end. One of the best examples is that of W. C. Handy, later known as the "Father of the Blues," whose career was launched on Beale Street. As Angela Davis establishes, blues emerged as the only form of music that "articulated a new valuation of individual emotional needs and desires" after slavery ended and Black people were free to leave the South, either by absolute necessity or out of their own desire to pursue opportunities inaccessible to them in the South. Beale Street and other similar areas of the Black South were locations where sexuality might be explored in a variety of ways. Kid Douglas knew that if she was to make a career out of her musical talent, staying close to Beale Street was her best option. She was right. As a member of the community of Black musicians, she received invaluable exposure to the more experienced guitarists and advice from people like Frank Stokes and Furry Lewis. There she honed her craft in a competitive and uncertain environment where "the majority [of musicians] lived from one night to the next."[11] One fellow musician remembered that Minnie "'was beginning to learn guitar and he was able to teach her a few things,' but before long, Minnie herself was the reigning blues queen of Memphis, and there was little she could learn from the competition."[12]

Her recording career began the summer of 1929 when a Columbia records talent scout was scouring Beale Street for musical talent and stumbled upon Kid Douglas performing in a barber shop with Joe McCoy. Her presence there shows her willingness to move beyond limits expected of respectable women and to take her place in spaces that were not meant for women, that were, in fact, dominated by men. Playing the blues brought her from the Jim Crow South to the North when they traveled to New York to record their first session in 1929. Perhaps basking in the bliss of their first major accomplishment, they married that same year. Leaving the South must have been challenging for the small-town girl who had been navigating Jim Crow restrictive spaces, but she would continue to travel to New York and Chicago.

Although her music was not released until 1930, she too was performing in the 1920s when other blues women, Ma Rainey, Bessie Smith, Sippie Wallace, Victoria Spivey, and Gladys Bentley, had been recording. Of these women, Daphne Duval Harrison argues that their music asserted "ideals from the standpoint of the working class and the poor." She observes further that studying their music "expands the base of knowledge about the role of black women in the creation and the development of American popular culture; illustrates their moves and means for coping successfully with gender-related discrimination and exploitation; and demonstrates an emerging model for the working woman—one who is sexually independent, self-sufficient, creative, assertive, and trend-setting."[13] Through the country blues she brought to the North and performed in different parts of the country, Minnie would add to and lengthen the conversation started by these women with her perspective of the "working woman."

A common theme in Minnie's music is wayward, lowdown men. The theme is often expressed in women's blues. Her life certainly gave her cause to sing on the subject, as she is thought to have married three times. Blues was prominent in one way or another with these relationships as each man was, like Memphis Minnie, a musician. The Garons question whether she was actually married to Will Weldon, known professionally as Casey Bill, who was a guitarist with the Memphis Jug Band, a group with which she recorded in 1935. Steve LaVere who knew her named Weldon as her first husband, but the Garons are skeptical, finding no evidence from people who knew her or any documentation of their relationship. There is evidence through eyewitnesses who corroborate that she was married (legally or through common-law marriage) to Kansas Joe McCoy and Ernest "Little Son Joe" Lawlars. What is clear is that Memphis Minnie enjoyed the company of men and was literally married to her music. There is little separation, if any, between the pleasure she enjoyed or even the frustrations she endured between her personal and professional lives. Like other blues women, her songs show the "aesthetic representations of [how] the politics of gender and sexuality are informed by and interwoven with their representations of race and class."[14] For Minnie, she used the blues to imagine better worlds, to build better communities, and to critique societies that were not safe for or respectful of Black women.

By the time she recorded her famous "Bumble Bee"[15] when she and McCoy went to Chicago in 1929, she had already become known by men for being able to hold her own artistically among them. Sometime in the 1930s they settled in the city and their performances in local clubs captured the attention of Black newspapers. One of her contemporaries, Booker T. Washington White, reminisced about her ability to own a performative space among men, "Memphis Minnie, Washboard Sam, Tampa Red, Big Bill, they were my favorite 'cause they really would knock the cover off a house. They play in the nightclubs. Would play house parties through the day."[16] Without question, there was something seductive and special about Memphis Minnie's performances that drew the attention and respect of men as she also intimidated them.

Minnie was not afraid to be seen naked, wanting, needing, longing. When Ma Rainey began recording in 1923, she opened the door for Black women blues singers to express their erotic pleasures in song. Davis notes that, "The overarching sexual themes that define the context of the blues form point the way toward a consideration of the historical politics of black sexuality."[17] Minnie followed their lead by writing and performing songs that spoke of her sexual interactions with men of her choosing. One of her most popular songs is "Bumble Bee," a blatantly sexual song that utilizes nature as a metaphor for mating and sexual passion. She sings, "Bumble Bee, bumble bee, please come back to me/He got the best old stinger any bumble bee that I ever seen/He stung me this morning/I been looking for him all day long." In the first nine lines, she establishes the bee as a male and acknowledges his ability to keep her longing for his stinger, or penis. Normally, a bee would be an unwanted presence as its sting causes pain, but the stinger she begs for brings her pleasure. Speaking to the essence of pleasure, Jerry Wasserman concludes, Memphis Minnie expressed that she is "concerned entirely with satisfying her own desire."[18] She sings on, "I can't stand to hear him buzz, buzz, buzz/ Come in, bumble bee, want you to stop your fuss." She indicates that he is as sexually attracted to her as she is to him. Their begging and longing for one another is mutual and she is willing to oblige his interest in her.

In some ways, she is stroking his sexual ego and this serves her to get what she wants from him. She claims him as hers, "You're my bumble bee and you know your stuff." This is not a romantic love song; it is about sexual satisfaction and her unapologetic interests in indulging her desires. Giving him freedom to leave as long as he knows that "you're needed here at home" is a compromise that keeps him returning to her bed. She ends by giving him permission to "Oh sting me bumble bee, until I get enough."[19] Minnie's blues persona is in control of her body as she chooses to submit to the man she has chosen to make her moan.

As the Garons point out, she recorded five different versions of "Bumble Bee" and they differ significantly from the original Columbia version. There are any number of reasons why the lyrics changed. One obvious one is to bring something new but familiar to her audience. Though the earliest recorded version was one of her signature songs that also captured the excitement of her budding career, Bumble Bee No. 2 is more sensual in her longing for the man to satisfy her. She twice repeats the line, "where you been so long . . . I been restless all day long." She tells of how he made her groan, "he made me cry for more." And then she emphasizes it by moaning "Hmmmm." Expressing her preference that he not leave so she can have "the honey I need" in a bungalow she will build just for them. She ends, "all I want now/my bumble bee just to stay at home."[20] The longing in this version is more intense; she shows vulnerability in response to his absences, which leads to her not receiving what she wants as long and as much as she wants from the only one who can satisfy her desires. This stinging can bring her sweet pleasure, but its temporary satisfaction leaves her in a state of lingering and wanting.

On the other hand, "New Bumble Bee" makes her feel good, but the problem is that he makes other women feel good too. She moves from joy in the first two stanzas to complaint in the third stanza:

He gets to flying and buzzing,
Stinging everybody he meets (2x)
Lord, I wonder why my bumble bee
want to mistreat it.

Then she lets out a moan "Hummm."[21]

When in the earlier versions she celebrated and luxuriated in the pleasure he elicited in her, now the new sting gives her pleasure and pain. She ends with her disappointment, "He's stinging somebody, everywhere he lands."[22] This move from renaming the song to point to how the bumble bee shows the "natural ways of a man," gives her agency. In this revision or another chapter in the bumble bee love story, she does not make the man a bee as she did in the first version, but in this one she specifically compares the man to a bee. But, as the Garons astutely note, "the subject of Minnie's various Bumble Bee songs is hardly the 'simple' bumble bee of house and garden, nor is it simply one of the many metaphors for a lover that we find in the blues."[23] Sex is intoxicating and it is empowering in these blues songs.

Notably, this version comes after she was an established blues artist. By the time it was recorded, she "had recorded 24 issued sides, she was becoming a seasoned professional in the recording studio."[24] According to Marcus Charles Tribbett, "Memphis Minnie recorded from about 1930 to 1960" and "through her life, her work, and her songs—engaged in resistance to class, racial and gender-based oppression; she lived her life fiercely, independently, and 'in your face.'"[25] There was pleasure and pain in the musical world that she occupied and operated in. To be sure, the fact that she had the microphone empowered her. What happens when the woman singer questions the use of the power? Memphis Minnie was recording in an industry that was dominated by male artists and male representatives. For her to ask why she was being mistreated by a man should come as no surprise, as she is most certainly singing about more than sexual gratification.

Memphis Minnie had a complicated relationship with music as her personal and professional lives intertwined. By 1939, she had split with McCoy and married her musical partner and lifelong companion. Son Joe, who became known as Little Son Joe in the music industry, had been born Ernest Lawlars in the small town of Hughes, Arkansas, on May 18, 1900. They may have met in Memphis after Son Joe had his first recording session in 1935 in Jackson, Mississippi. Although Memphis Minnie was more advanced in her career, Son Joe was a guitarist, vocalist, and songwriter who complemented her work. With Son Joe by her side, her popularity would grow in the 1940s. According to the Garons, "Son Joe not only provided Minnie with solid backing, but did so imaginatively and with skill."[26] With him, she found the pleasure of song and the pleasure of love.

Finding varying levels of satisfaction in her personal and professional lives may have been inspiring. She consistently played with the idea of pleasure as empowering. At times, Minnie's blues persona bragged about her sexual allure. "Ice Man" is one of the boldest of these brag sessions. The song begins with a short guitar solo, announcing her presence. With confidence, she lyrically announces that she has multiple men and plans for each: "I've got a ice man in the spring, cold man in the fall, all I need now to get my ice[s] home." Bringing attention to herself and her ability to accomplish this, she repeats the line, "I'm going to strut my stuff."

Minnie brings attention to her body as a subject of power with the refrain, "I'm going to strut my stuff . . . everywhere I go." As a statement, it is a declaration of self-confidence in her ability to attract a man and to get him to do what she wants to meet her needs. Returning to the description by the Garons of her being a wild teenager, L. H. Stallings sees wildness as a quality worth analysis. Stallings states, "Wildness is radical Black female subjectivity that consciously celebrates autonomy and self-assertion in the invention process of self."[27] Minnie's celebration of self is clear in her telling the object of her desire that he can "Come on up, if you start anything, I'm going to strut my stuff everywhere I go." Strutting is an expression of feminine power. In the absence of her opinion of how she navigated the world in which she lived, Minnie creates a self that tells how she used her body as a form of action and pursuit, rather than one of hoping and languishing. This is about how to take control in an effort to solve a problem. Minnie's songs tell of her deliberate moving that involves "strutting her stuff." The Garons write, "there is one aspect of this appeal that deserves amplification: her visual allure and attractiveness." They go on, "The fact that Minnie did not refer to her own visual appeal sets her apart from so many other blues women, who in their songs often referred to their own good looks."[28] Instead, Minnie does not rely on how she is perceived based on her visual appearance; rather, she takes pleasure in her ability to entice or seduce men just by walking past one or strutting. She changes the script of women's blues from a man who has to make a decision based on how she looks to a man who cannot resist her allure.

The unnamed Ice Man is an example. He is a potential lover, but there are rules to the relationship that she clarifies. One of the most important is that if he gets rough, he will suffer for it physically: "If you start anything, I'm going to strut my stuff." In this, she declares ownership of her body and her right to withdraw consent. Again, she asserts her own power to move on from him and to take another lover.

The song shifts to reveal the significance of the "ice man," one who delivered ice that could be used for the preservation of perishable foods. Here we find that the song, as the title suggests, is about what the ice man can provide, the product of ice. In the absence of a refrigerator, an item of luxury not common to the working class, she is calling attention to a consumable need. The ice man sells ice, needed to preserve food and to provide comfort during hot days. Finally, she tells him that she ain't got no money. "Ice Man" uncovers the challenges of the working class and the lack of access to necessities. Erin Chapman concludes, "the blues-woman was in many ways emblematic of all black women."[29] "Ice Man" is not just about a woman flaunting her sexuality; it is also about her need for the man to fulfill her desire for a product she cannot afford.

"My Strange Man" is yet another example of her unapologetic declaration for sex. Most certainly, this song not only shows her as the aggressor but also shows how she relishes the exercise of choice. After a musical interlude her lone voice sings, "I met a strange man last night, and I'm taking him home with me." For emphasis she repeats, "I met a strange man last night, and I took him home with me." To take home meant something to the audience. Saidiya Hartman asserts, "The tenement and the rooming house furnished the social laboratory of the black working class and the poor. The bedroom was a domain of thought in deed and site for enacting, exceeding, undoing, and remaking relations of power."[30] Minnie's home, whether it is in Chicago, Memphis, or some other place in her travels, is a place where her power unfolds.

After the declaration, she admits that her choice of bringing him home with her does not grant her absolute control of him, as he has choices as well. "Now he don gone and left me, wondering where my strange man can be?" "Strange Man" vacillates. It is a song that tests the power of gendered subjects. She moves from feeling empowered by the declaration of the fact of his coming home with her to wondering where he went while she was sleeping. "Strange Man, strange man won't you please come back to me." She declares, he is her strange man and that he has something she really needs. Moaning is repeated twice. Her desire for him and the pain of not being able to make him stay leaves her without words that the moaning fills.

Upon his return, she asks him where he has been but she truthfully confesses that she is "happy" he returned. Minnie may be enamored with the man's presence in her life, but she is clear to define her expectations. The song ends with her telling him "the next time you leave me, I'm a walk out and lock my door." By acknowledging that he will leave her, she also affirms that she will end the relationship by "locking my door." The door represents her idea of not having further intimacies and of not allowing him access to her home. In this, Minnie calls out what is hers. The man comes to her home, where she is in charge. Likewise, she proclaims possession of her body and the choice to let him have access to it or not.

Minnie issues an invitation to no one in particular in "Ain't Nobody Home But Me," but it is clear that she is talking to a man about visiting her for sexual gratification. She sings gaily, "Come on home, any time, ain't nobody there but me." Davis observes of the sexual tensions in blues, "One of the most obvious ways in which blues lyrics deviated from that era's established popular musical culture was their provocative and pervasive sexual . . . imagery."[31] As if speaking to a man who may be put off or confused by what she is saying, she eases into her meaning with each phrase. First, she reassures him by saying, "Don't be scared. Your momma's gonna cook you a nice fat duck" and a "shimmy" will occur. Shimmying could refer to a dance or any form of seductive gyrations. She assures him further that she is alone and perhaps lonely, but most certainly wants his company, because "Ain't nobody there but me." As she goes on, she becomes more obviously sexual by telling him to "Bring your mama a nice big banana."

The upswing rhythm made by the piano arrangement shows that this is a song written to have fun. It calls for movement by the listener as Minnie invites a man to respond to her innuendos from one declaration to the next. The final reference to the banana and sitting on a piano places the music and lyrics together to accentuate the meaning of what she is hoping for. The two move together toward a rather clever climax that complements the performance of Minnie as singer, songwriter, and performer who is interacting with her accompanist. It is her voice that takes the lead and guides the willing listener.

"Black Cat Blues," where she sings, "Everybody wants to buy my kitty," works similarly as a song that speaks of self-gratification, and, possibly prostitution. On one hand, the kitty refers to her sexual allure and her success in keeping a man of substance of three years. Although the kitty is thought to be about her vagina, she changes the meaning along with the gaze. The black cat or kitty has more to do with her satisfaction and happiness than with a physical part of her body. Black cats are typically associated with bad luck, but this cat catches rats and "closes holes." The Garons observe, "Black Cat Blues is ostensibly about the virtues of a rat-catching cat. Although the third verse is ambiguous and the fifth is directly sexual. Minnie may have omitted mention of voodoo, bad luck or witchcraft, but ignoring these relevant attributes of black cats is entirely insufficient to suppress them."[32] Minnie's persona resists suppression. She also takes the black cat around with her everywhere she goes, showing a need to flaunt the object of her satisfaction but also to keep an eye on him. Yet, there is a suggestion by branding the satisfaction as a black cat, that there will be sadness as a result of the cat's presence in her life. For now, no one can take what she has deemed as hers.

In fact, folkloric beliefs that existed in Black southern communities but other communities as well made a series of her songs somewhat relatable to audiences of all backgrounds. From "Black Cat Blues" to "Bad Luck Blues," Memphis Minnie gave voice to struggles and challenges of being a working-class Black woman and considered what it could look like to change her trying circumstances. "Bad Luck Blues" speaks more specifically to a suggestion that she is in a constant battle with fate and her own choices. Bad luck is a hindrance to pleasure. Minnie laments the cycle of having and then not having. It is a classic blues song in the sense that it is, what Ralph Ellison termed simply as, a "complaint." Yet, it is, perhaps, a bait and switch. There is a series of men. The first gets sick and dies. The second worked hard and then became her man and lost his "doggone" job. Her descriptions of the men and why they are no longer together are reflections of society and their impact on the men, and her by extension. Yet, she also resists being a victim of a racist society and its impact on Black men. There is also a possibility that she is expressing resistance to men who are not up to standard, as we know that Minnie wrote of exchanges for her time and body.

Minnie consistently critiques the idea of masculinity as it relates to violence and sexual ability. The next man was tall and turned out to be violent. Asserting herself, she rejects him, suggesting that she does not desire to be with a "rough man," as is also expressed to the Ice Man. Following the tall man, she says she had a short and fat man who "couldn't keep it tight like that." She asks the question, "I'm a bad luck woman, I can't see the reason why." Here the relationship ends because the man is not able to satisfy her in one way or another. The term *keeping it fit* follows a description of his size; yet, listeners may infer what exactly was not fit, his sexual abilities or his waistline or perhaps both.

Singing showed a feminine vulnerability that contrasted greatly with the violent woman that fellow blues artists described as knowing. Their Memphis Minnie handled men roughly and left them in awe. With her husband, Son Joe, Johnnie Shines heard that "she just worked him over when she felt like it." Like the imagined or reimagined characters and contrived events that they sang about, Memphis Minnie was the subject of unproven tales. Shine's admittance that he "heard" how she treated her husband extended to her being the same woman who "shot one old man's arms off, down in Mississippi. Shot his arm off, or cut it off with a hatchet."[33] He concluded, "Minnie was a hellraiser."[34] Such mythical antics show how the woman survived in a culture that favored men and their masculine bravado. Memphis Minnie's voice would, in many ways, challenge what people thought about her. But as her musical persona took on many identities, she indulged these myths and tales in her music, much to the delight of her fans.

In "I'm a Bad Luck Woman," she points to her desire for good and the absence of bad, but curiously, she names herself as the "bad luck woman," and not that she has bad luck. There is a suggestion here that there is no ridding herself of the "bad," an experience that she would know as a Black woman trying to make her way in 1930s America. Bad plagues her life, hinders loving relationships, and challenges Black masculinity. Memphis Minnie appears to indict racism and its impact on Black people's search for peace in their homes, prosperity through labor, and love among themselves.

Therefore, having a partner who is willing to share in the struggle for survival is important, as she makes clear in "Man You Don't Give Me Nothing." The song is an indictment of masculinity as expected of men. If a man is unable to provide her with the things that she wants and that we may presume he has promised, then why keep him in her life? As a song that clearly sees gender roles of women and men different than the other, she tells the man, "You won't give me no money, you won't give me no clothes to wear. Tell me man, what do you expect for the poor women's to do?" But the song is not about the man giving to her; rather, she indicts him for trying to "take her for a fool" by expecting her to give him her money and then leaving. By asking him, "What did he learn in school?" she imposes on him his lack of acknowledging an expectation that she is there to help ("No I don't mind helping"), but that she not be the sole provider. In this, Minnie asserts her independence as well as her insistence that their relationship be one where she is respected as a partner. To accept any other way of living would make her a fool. These songs act as responses to songs by men of being providers of things women like and need. Hers is an indictment of the lack of satisfaction she feels with them, which disrupts any hope she may have to enjoy pleasure.

In her personal life, Minnie is known to have expressed expectations of her man, leaving her vulnerable to criticism. Jimmy Rogers referred to her as "real bitchy" and goes on to describe one night in which she saw Son Joe "talking and drinking" in the presence of other women.[35] Apparently angered by his comfort and delight, she rushed over, grabbed his drink, and threw it in his face. When next Rogers saw Son Joe, he was wearing sunglasses to shield his wounded eyes. Rogers admits that she was kind to him and never saw her injure Son Joe again. There is no context provided here. Listeners of his tale have no way of knowing what may have prompted Memphis Minnie. Though Rogers may see this as an unreasonable act, she may very well have been expressing a need—perhaps a much-repeated need—for respect. Nevertheless, the two remained together until Son Joe's death in 1961.

The blues phenome was "a tough, hard drinking woman in a crowd of tough, hard working men."[36] As a woman who moaned about her sexual exploits and who could play the guitar with men accompanists, Memphis Minnie was often compared to the men who dominated the blues; indeed, she was in the minority among her peers. This was the consequence of crossing gender and genre boundaries. Tribbett offers, "Minnie doesn't fit easily into the country blues camp because she did not record in the twenties."[37] Booker T. Washington White's description of her playing with men and "knocking the cover off the house" places her as the only woman in the company of male blues artists. In other words, she was judged as having earned her place on the sacred blues stage.

Consequently, she always seemed to have to be placed within the performative blues space, which was considered masculine. In his brief description of her as "one of the greatest of all of the women singers of the 30's, or of any other period," Giles Oakley sees her voice as a contradiction of sound and body: "her voice had authority and distinction." Oakley echoes that of Hughes's assessment of Minnie. "The electric guitar is very loud, science having magnified all the softness away. Memphis Minnie sings through a microphone and her voice—hard and strong anyhow for a little woman's is made harder and stronger by scientific sound."[38] Besides accentuating her style of performance, I illuminate Hughes's move toward accentuating her femininity. The "softness" of the "little woman" is accented by Hughes who tries to save her from the "loud science" of the instruments.[39] Tribbett goes further by drawing attention to her masculine ways, noting "she is described, both by the performers who knew her and heard stories of her and by critics who have written after her death, as a tough-as-nails woman who could take care of herself. She actively cultivated and maintained this reputation throughout her career, one hears it in her songs, and it persists posthumously in blues criticism." Indeed, the Garons provide testimonies of men who "heard" that she fought other men.[40] Artist Homesick James, declared, "That woman was tougher than a man."[41] What she may have been reacting to or why is not a part of these testimonies. Several songs, such as "Gambling Woman," "You Ain't Done Nothing to Me," and "Moonshine Blues" speak to her "toughness" in the blues world that she creates and the real world that she critiques or at least her willingness to resist forms of oppression.

In "I'm a Gambling Woman" she positions herself among men and in opposition to them. She describes winning so much money, she "got to take back her mojo." Again, she calls on folkloric beliefs to explain her circumstances. In this case, she has good luck or mojo that brings her money she surely needs to take care of her financial obligations. There is pleasure in winning. As described by her peers, Minnie was known for gambling and according to her, "I gamble everywhere I go." Winning makes her feel powerful. By the time she came to Beale Street, it was known to have "gambling spots, both high and low," where "such sharks as Slop Crowder, Casino Henry"[42] and others were known to set up shop. If she was gambling with men, she could outwit them and take their money rather than to rely on one of them to give her money. Her presence then, disrupts a male-dominated space and places her in a position of power outside her home where she usually finds her dominant voice.

There is a risk to a relationship when a woman pursues pleasure among men who are not her lover. Minnie sings about the joy and the consequence of enjoyment: "I gambled all last night, all last night before. I win so much money, I start to take back my mojo. I shot craps all last night until the break of day." Her man ran away when she returned. There is a suggestion here that her success was too much for him to handle. Her moaning laments the loss of her lover. Minnie's position as "the man" is part of her story and her reputation, as the Garons and others have reported.

If people created the "bitchy" Minnie persona, she would embrace the image in her blues. Indeed, she was a gambling woman and this was dangerous territory to navigate. She revels in it as she does in "Moonshine." Here she tells the story of why she won't sell the illegal substance any more. Moonshine, or homemade whiskey, was illegal to make for the purpose of sale. Perhaps the allure was the illegality of it or the danger associated with drinking and selling it, but it brings trouble that is the making of an upbeat song. Or, this song could very well have been the indulgence of a pleasure. Minnie was known for enjoying Wild Irish Rose and corn whiskey. She sings, "I've got to leave this town, I got to go before the sun go down. Because I don got caught and the coppers running me around."

In fact, in a rare moment, she expresses regret for her actions. Minnie says that when she leaves she won't sell moonshine no more. Freedom comes in the travel. She sings, "I don packed up my trunk and shipped it down the road. I don made up in my mind I won't sell moonshine no more." Minnie does not say why she was selling liquor, but the presence of the police invokes a clear fear in capture and whatever else may happen if she is caught. When she sings of gambling, this is a community affair that she brags about, even though it brings some tension to her relationship. However, the feeling of control that leads to a feeling of exhilaration contrasts greatly with her interaction with the police. This is a kind of danger that could lead to violence enacted by a powerful government entity. Jail is not a place this Black woman wants to be.

Yet, selling moonshine, like gambling, brought to the song's persona and others involved money that they otherwise may not have had. The risk is great, but with such few choices, she and her "daddy" (reference to her lover) found themselves willing to take the chance that could mean surviving just one more day. Minnie's song may resonate with the people who find themselves just trying to survive, but by making such choices they find themselves arrested, impoverished, and working in prison fields or on chain gangs. Minnie may sing of leaving and relishing the freedom of packing and running, but what will she do when she gets to her next destination, is the question that lingers for the blues listeners.

Her songs assert feminine power as a way of accessing pleasure. Issuing a direct warning to a wayward man in "Good Morning," she says, "Good morning, tell me where you stayed last night." We can imagine that the man has just come in and is being greeted with this command. There is a contrast here between the pleasant greeting of "good morning" and the terse statement that is not an inquiry, "tell me." The lover is given a command and not a request. Beginning this way presents Minnie as one who is not using a tone of pleading for attention as in "New Bumble Bee." In fact, the faster rhythm of the song does not leave space for moans of sadness. It moves and leads and the lover like the listener moves in anticipation of what may happen when the answer comes.

Again, she does not ask, she tells him, "You know you just don't love me and you just can't treat me right." She goes on to declare the truth as she believes it, "It's a lowdown shame, the way you treated me." This declaration shows that she is telling her song, the story of how she perceives the relationship. By not asking the lover, if he loves her and why he does not treat her right, she will not allow him the opportunity to interrupt or to amend what she has come to conclude. Minnie is in control of her story.

Not being a fool emerges as a common theme as well. In "Hoodoo Lady" Minnie celebrates the power of women as women. She simultaneously requests and proclaims, "Don't put that thang on me, cause I'm going back to Tennessee." Minnie suggests here that the Hoodoo Lady has an ability to change the course of events for the better or for the good. Hoodoo, in this context, is in reference to Black people's beliefs that a female practitioner could use earthly elements to connect with the supernatural world with an intent on having some control over the environment in which they live. The Hoodoo Lady is to be feared, as Minnie says in her closing line. Ultimately, Minnie does not want her ability to move from where she is, perhaps Chicago or wherever she may have been performing this song at any moment, to hinder her from going back to her home. Davis sees the connection between blues and freedom: "What is distinctive about the blues, however, particularly in relation to other American popular musical forms of the 1920s and 1930s, is their intellectual independence and representational freedom."[43] Travel signifies independence and freedom; as far as Minnie is concerned, she wants the Hoodoo Lady to help her to achieve that goal and not to hinder it.

Her awesome and unique talent is also wanted by a woman who has needs that she does not have the ability to make materialize. Minnie, therefore, has requests of the Hoodoo Lady. She asks her "to unlock my door so I can go in and get all my clothes." Listeners do not know why the singer does not have access to her belongings. Was she locked out by the landlord? Was she kicked out by a man? Anything is possible in the working-class world that Minnie represents. Whatever the case, she sees the Hoodoo Lady as having the ability to improve her circumstances and grant her the ability to "unlock" doors that have been closed to her because of her gender or class or some other reason. The Hoodoo Lady is capable of crossing barriers.

As is usual for her songs, Minnie does not hesitate to speak of her sexual desires for a man. As if in conversation with another woman who too would have such needs and, therefore, understands and may sympathize with Minnie, she asks the Hoodoo Lady to "Bring my man back home but don't let him stay all night." The man's presence is needed for temporary gratification, but not for a long period of time. With the Lady's help, Minnie can have what she wants and for as long as she wants.

The use of the word *lady* as opposed to *woman* suggests that the woman is seen as respectable by Minnie. She even compares her to Jesus in her ability to manipulate natural elements: "You can turn water to wine." Yet, there is a presence of mistrust that Minnie has for the Hoodoo Lady because "She's tricky as she can be." Minnie also repeats her plea that she not "put that thang on me." Describing her as a complex being with duality, Minnie sees her power as (mis)gendered in the sense that she can do what a revered biblical man can do, but because of that she is also feared. Minnie, who was also seen as a complex woman of duality, may have understood the Hoodoo Lady. In the blues world, gender roles are not strictly defined. They are tested and depend strongly on the context of the figure. The Hoodoo Lady's power is extended to Minnie, which makes her powerful as well.

One of the best songs in her corpus that illuminates her own power as a resilient woman is "You Ain't Done Nothing to Me." Her lyrics are simple and repetitive. Repetition serves to reiterate a point and to put emphasis on the main point. For her, it is clear, her lover can do any number of things to her that may be attempts to scare or humiliate her, but she will not empower those attempts. Through this song, Minnie shows that power is only seen as such if someone acknowledges an act as having an effect or an influence that results in an outcome that makes the person who has been perceived as not having power as being unable to ignore or not acknowledge the attempt as powerful. Minnie does not acknowledge the man she is addressing as powerful, even as she gives one example after the other of his attempt to intimidate or control her. She begins with money, a symbol of power that can be used to control a person who does not have any. She declares, "You may take every dime I've got, but you can't do nothing to me." She goes on, he may withhold his companionship, "You may drive me from your door," but this has no effect because "You can't do nothing to me."

Emphasis is important as she moves from "you ain't" to "you can't." She sings, "It don't make no difference what you may do, you can't do nothing to me." Use of "you ain't" acknowledges a failed attempt. Once it has been established that the attempts are not working to sway her opinion of his actions, she moves to "you can't." This final proclamation means that he does not possess the ability to dominate her.

Minnie also sees his attempts from a gendered point of view and dismisses this as well. She sings, "You may cock your pistol in my face, but you ain't done nothing to me." Pistol here can be a reference to a gun or it can be a reference to his penis. Either way, she uses the pistol as a phallic symbol to tell him that his masculinity is inept in making her fear him. As she moves toward the end, she emphasizes her resolve, a position that she does not sway from, by adding "ah" and "oh." More specifically, "Ah, you can't do nothing to me." "Oh, you can't do nothing to me. You may kick me." One of her final lines, she tells him "I'm talking to you." Minnie insists that her voice be heard and that ignoring her is not an option for the man.

To be sure, Minnie is explaining why her persona is willing to be in a relationship with a man who has or may be doing the things that she describes in the song. Some of the lines may be exaggeration, if you do this, then know that this will not affect me. But, the message is clear, she is making a choice to remain and how she will remain. Minnie is singing about who she is in relation to what is happening. She is in control of her actions and reaction to her circumstances and whatever the man takes, he cannot make her feel or not feel any certain way.

Feeling powerful does not render a woman incapable of feeling lonely. Memphis Minnie reminds us that pleasure is not consistent or finite. Minnie's persona in "Lonesome Song" shows her vulnerability as a woman who is not in access of pleasure. "I woke up this morning with a feeling, and I feel I've been had all day long. Going from door to door singing the same old lonesome song." Minnie expresses acute blues that has been brought on by a man who leaves her feeling as though she is simply not good enough. In a direct address to the missing man, as if writing him a letter, she reveals his perspective based on how he has treated her, "I never do anything right." His ability to affect her mood is obvious and she does not try to hide how his lack of attention to her desire to feel wanted makes her feel. Minnie gives in to her desire to be fulfilled by the man. If they are to be together, she wants him to be truthful. She then asks, "Please tell me how long you will be gone . . . You can't fool me, I know there is something goin on wrong. You be so late coming home." Minnie envisions equitability by asking him to talk to her.

However, there is a turn in this song or a part B to the story. Minnie has a plan. She shares, "When I get my money, I'm going to stop this lonesome song. It's going to be goodbye daddy." Minnie suggests that at least one reason why she is with him is because she is financially depended on the man. Unlike some of the other songs, the man is providing her with basic needs. However, for this Minnie, it is not enough. Good-bye contrasts with her going door to door singing a lonesome song. If Minnie is trapped in this relationship because of her financial situation and emotional dependence, she sees a way out. Rather than lamenting his absence, she reminds him and perhaps herself that she can leave him and put an end to her misery. This turn to a plan of escape shows Minnie taking back her power and treating him the way that she has been treated. He will wonder where she is once she is gone.

"Good Morning" is part of a long conversation that expresses frustration from a woman scorned. As she does in "You Ain't Done Nothing to Me," she informs him that his actions will not sway what is to come. She sings, "You can shoot your pistol, you can blow your horn, you can fall down on your knees . . . And you gon be sorry you treated me this way." Circling back to "Lonesome Song," she tells him he will feel lonesome when their relationship is over and, to be clear, she is informing him that there is no reason for her to keep him around. Minnie presents a voice that is unwavering in changing her circumstances by taking control of her distressing situation.

Lastly, she demands a confession. "Good morning might as well be good bye," she sings. But, she clarifies that she still wants him to tell her where he stayed last night. Based on the legend of Memphis Minnie, her interest may be in confronting the person that took her lover's attention, for it is possible that she has her suspicions. Whatever the reasons, there is a measure of humor in cursing the man for his "lowdown ways" and then asking him, again, "tell me where you were." Pleasure comes in the form of the demand to know where he was, the promise of a bleak future for the wayward lover, and then her final insistence that he respond.

Mistreatment can be seen as a form of masculine control as she expresses in "I Don't Want You No More." She opens with the reason for the end of this relationship, that she has come home in the morning and found another woman wearing her gown. Never mind the fact that she was not home that night, Minnie labels the man as having "ways [that] are too lowdown." Lowdown is used often in her songs and was a common way of referring to people who mistreat others without regard for the other person's feelings. In keeping with the frequent use of double entendre in blues music, it could also refer to, in this context, a man who is trying to keep her low or without. She sings that he doesn't want to "see me with a nickel in my hand."

"Want" speaks to desire. Minnie says, "I don't want you no more." Therefore, the man's "lowdown ways" have brought her to a point where she no longer desires him. She tells her lover that he should find another woman and she will find another man. Minnie, then, expresses that her desire is for a man who uplifts her rather than tries to hinder her in some way. Keeping in mind that these songs were written in the mid-1930s, having to live in a society where there was extreme racial prejudice and gender inequality, especially during the Great Depression, being in a relationship with a man who brings her "low," emotionally and financially, is unacceptable. Minnie resists any idea of being in a personal situation where she must deal with conflicts that exacerbate the public struggles she has as a Black woman.

Minnie did not always sing about relationships or interactions with men. Lonesomeness could come in the form of a lack of support from members of the community. As noted, many of her songs make at least a slight reference to a lack of money. Perhaps a man is not giving her any, she may be working and the man is taking the money, or she does not have any to even pay the ice man. "Out in the Cold" speaks to what happens when she wakes up homeless. This song surely resonated with so many suffering from the effects of the Depression.

Dreams can be insightful and wishful. Minnie presents no hope in "Out in the Cold": "I dreamt a dream last night, I never dreamt before . . . I didn't have no money didn't have no place to go. Why didn't you let me in? The reason I sure don't know. Up and down this old lonesome road. Which a way must I go?" In her description of how it feels to walk around in the cold and to be ignored by others who can see and hear her moaning, she moans, to make her voice heard. Moaning can be a cry of ecstasy at a higher octave, but the lower register is unmistakable pain. Minnie expresses what it is like to plead for understanding, only to be made invisible.

Minnie uses her voice to bring attention to the ignored. During the era of the Depression, the blues were appropriate as an expression of the needy. People stood in long lines for small amounts of food to feed themselves and other members of the families. The jobless rate was high, especially for unskilled workers. Minnie and her lovers were in the music industry that relied on sales of albums and people's willingness to pay a fee for a live performance. She provided an escape as she herself escaped from the grueling work of field work in the rural South. This song captures the spirit of generosity that she reportedly extended as a mentor and friend to other musicians. Their community was complicated, but they relied on one another to survive. In this vein, Minnie issues a call for the community to do what it can for one another.

Early Black blues musicians received very little compensation for their work. Once they reached an age when they no longer traveled and could no longer perform, they had to rely on others. Unable to maintain her independence, Memphis Minnie's sisters took care of her. Son Joe died from health complications. Minnie suffered from strokes and was eventually left in the care of a nursing facility under the supervision of her sisters who ensured that she was properly dressed for the fans who visited her. The legend's songs continued to be recorded and fans sent her money when they learned of the modest income that she received from social security.

During the era of the Depression, Memphis Minnie moved from the rural South to the urban South and later to the North to establish a remarkable career that kept her performing and traveling through the 1960s. Hers was an important voice for working-class, sexually expressive Black women at a time in which the country was preoccupied with moving past a financial crisis. Within the lyrics and harmony of her musical art, we find what L. H. Stallings describes as a "self-authored sexual desire and radical Black female sexual subjectivity that purposely incorporates that desire as the context for rebellion from the beginning, as opposed to its presence as an afterthought."[44] Through her songwriting, guitar-playing, and soulful singing, Memphis Minnie served as a social critic who gave rise to a new and emerging style of the blues that brought pleasure to her as an artist, but most of all her career captures the rise of a Black woman who took the chance to make a life that existed beyond boundaries.

5

Pleasurable Resistance in Langston Hughes's *Not Without Laughter*

Langston Hughes was a voyeur of Black women. His observations of Black women and friendships with them led to written tapestries in the forms of newspaper articles, fiction, poetry, and plays. Black women, such as those discussed, were muses for Hughes's art; from them he leaned in and listened to the stories they told with a multitude of performances, from their gospel and blues songs, stoop or barroom stories, public declarations of love, and stage or street dances. In them, Hughes searched for the beautiful tenor of Black life, borne from sadness, fatigue, and a little bit of daring unapologetic joy.

Published in 1930, Langston Hughes's *Not Without Laughter: A Novel* features the lives of four African American women described primarily from the perspective of a boy named Sandy. Starting from the age of eight until he is sixteen years old, Sandy observes the struggles of women in his family. Sandy's parenting is inconsistent. He is the son of Jimboy, a traveling blues musician, and Annjee, a domestic laborer who eventually abandons her son to pursue her wandering husband. Like Hughes when he was a child, Sandy lives with his grandmother, who is the center of stability in his life. Aunt Hagar is the family's Christian matriarch who is respected by her White and Black neighbors of Stanton, Kansas. Born in slavery, she developed a close relationship with her White mistress who died by suicide and, as a result, Hagar holds no hatred toward Whites; instead, she regards them as she would anyone—some are good and some are bad. Aunt Hagar is a proud Baptist washerwoman guided by Christian principles, and it is those beliefs that create tension between her and her three daughters, Harriet/Harrie, Tempy, and Annjee/Annjelica.

Aunt Hagar is a model for Black respectability, a way of surviving that she developed during her time as an enslaved woman—when Black individuals' control of their bodies was superseded by the desires (indeed legal ownership) of White owners. In contrast, Hughes presents readers with an outright criticism of Black respectability by offering a counter perspective that negates a White ideal of desire and advances a Black idea that defines pleasure as freedom from sexual, social, creative, and political confinement. Pursuing pleasure as freedom provides the women with an opportunity to define themselves—who they are, what they want, and why they want it. In this chapter, I am interested in emphasizing how Hughes achieves this presentation of pleasure despite the level of influence exerted by his patron Charlotte Osgood Mason. Critiquing Christian principles derived from the practices of enslavers, Hughes represents the desire for freedom in the movement of the body as Black political resistance. Pursuit of pleasure is intensely personal and, as Michael Nylan notes, trying to divert a person from pursuing pleasure is futile.[1] Annjee, Jimboy, and Harriet are perfect exemplars of this argument, as they exercise futility. Erin Chapman argues that instead of respectability, Hughes, among others, "touted a radical individualism and independence from all but the most personal allegiances to 'art' or 'self' or some other self-generated ideal."[2] Influenced by his observations and interactions with Black women, especially his mother, Hughes presents Black women's pleasure as an expression of the woman's self.

Aunt Hagar's daughters possess a desire to exist beyond the confines of Stanton, the home place that has few opportunities for Black people, other than working for Whites. In doing so, the novel emphasizes Black people's right to have "fun" as a metaphor for pleasure. Fun—a word he uses to describe his love of Black folks to his father—is Black individual's exercise of agency. It is an embrace of a choice, for good or for bad. Two of the women's relationships with fun-loving Jimboy give them access to their quieted desire for pleasure. Both Harriet and Jimboy use performance to cross social boundaries that are set to suppress a myriad of gendered desires, including sexual and artistic. As a Black man, Jimboy insists that he enjoy the freedom of moving about as he pleases. Although his decision severely limits his role as a father, as a Black individual he finds freedom of movement as part of his masculine privilege. Boundaries that mark freedom of movement as strictly masculine are challenged by Harriet. In contrast to Jimboy, Harriet is a woman who is expected to stay home, stay away from men, and contribute to the family by working a respectable job. Her love of the blues allows her to move past these gendered boundaries. Such boundary crossing brings Harriet in possession of the sexuality that her mother wants her to suppress; and when Harriet resists suppression she finds a kind of social power that benefits her first and then her family.

My focus in this chapter is to examine how Hughes presents pleasure as a form of resistance to his perception of respectability. Drawing from his personal observations of Black women as public performers, including the women I discussed in the preceding chapters, Hughes created women with distinct personalities that enhanced his ability to tease out the meaning of private desires as they are explored in public spaces. Such acts are forbidden under the strain of respectable Christian behavior, but Hughes asks a question of "What if?" What if a Black woman chooses to live a life she wants without making the advancement of the race her priority? For Hughes, then, desire is expressed in rebellious acts that are both conscious and unconscious and that show a willingness to move beyond prescribed boundaries.

Aunt Hagar's three daughters, Harriet, Tempy, and Annjee are vastly different women that give Hughes the space to press his readers to consider the meaning of suppression in the lives of African Americans. Tempy, or Temperance, as her name suggests, is a cold, prim, and proper Episcopalian who shuns her family and comes just in time to save her nephew, Sandy, when her mother dies, so that she can make him into a respectable credit to the race. Her demeanor and outright hatred of anything that is too Black, like blues music and rambunctious Baptist church services, contrasts with the lifestyle and interests of her younger sister Harriet. Harriet's pursuit of pleasure through performing blues—a genre that speaks to a truth of life as she knows it—is a form of resistance to her mother's generational sense of respectability that is now her sister Tempy's way of life. Lastly, Annjee's love of fun-loving, guitar-playing, irresponsible Jimboy turns her from a woman in love to a woman in alienation because of love lost. At the heart of this novel is a question about respectability. Who defines respectability in working-class Black communities and from one generation to the next? Is the definition, in fact, fluid, depending on the definer? How does respectability clash with Black women's agency and the pursuit of a Black female self? Each woman grapples with these questions.

Hughes's novel is distinctly inspired by his childhood and influenced by his love of his grandmother and Black performance. In the absence of his father and mother, Hughes lived with his maternal grandmother in Lawrence, Kansas, until the woman's death in 1912. She provided the only stable home for him during his childhood as his mother, Carrie Hughes Clark, pursued an acting career and a relationship with her second husband who moved often. Ten years after *Not Without Laughter* was published, he would describe his childhood in *The Big Sea*. His grandmother was a devout Christian. For her, if she attained any level of pleasure, it was derived from what she did for others and her personal relationship with God. Conveyances of Christian grandmothers are common subjects in Black art. Hall Johnson and many other authors drew inspiration from their grandmothers, as teaching them "what it meant . . . [to] work until she 'got happy.'"[3] To "get happy" refers to a communing with the Holy Spirit that is part of a praise and worship by a person who believes that God has shown His favor on the person, despite any circumstances the person may be facing at the time. Johnson saw his grandmother's "humming, singing, and 'ecstatic shouts' [as influencing] his sense of the connection between religious experience and music."[4] In other words, working can bring pleasure and draw the worker closer to God. Aunt Hagar strives to please God by working hard, raising children that acknowledge Him, and praising Him at church and during revival. Long suffering and obedience are the burdens she carries, but her daughters seek not to inherit the same.

Aunt Hagar's daughter Tempy is an extreme example of what occurs when Black women pursue respectability over pleasure. Tempy is a woman who has, in her opinion, moved well past the humble beginnings of her working-class background thanks to a White woman. She had been exposed to whiteness and rewarded well for what the narrator says is her "worship of it." Mrs. Barr-Grant, "for whom she had worked for years as a personal maid," willed her small houses to Tempy because she pleased her "by being prompt and exact in obeying orders and by appearing to worship her Puritan intelligence."[5] She recalls that Mrs. Barr-Grant told her it was too bad that she was not White[6] and Tempy took this as a compliment. Her acceptance of Mrs. Barr-Grant gave her a way to navigate the burden of her being Black and poor in America during segregation. The whiter she could convey, the easier her life could be. Her embrace of whiteness may be a form of submission as much as it may be a form of resistance to any belief that Blacks could not achieve more than they had been allowed to according to the restrictions of racial discrimination. In any case, Hughes shows little respect for the women that Tempy represents.

Tempy's upper-class status gave her cause to uplift the race as she also believed that whiteness should be the standard for measuring uplift. From Hughes's perspective, we see a profile of an exaggerated version of an upper-class club woman as one who appears to despise all forms of blackness. In considering why taking custody of Sandy after her mother dies is important, she thinks, "Colored people needed to encourage talent so that the White race would realize Negroes weren't all mere guitar-players and house-maids. And Sandy would be a credit if he were raised right. Of course, Tempy knew he hadn't had the correct environment to begin with—living with Jimboy and Harriet and going to a Baptist church."[7] The national Black clubwomen's movement emerged in the late 1800s as a cluster of local clubs dedicated to uplifting formerly enslaved people from lowly social positions to more distinguished ones. Those who were more educated certainly saw themselves as servants, as Mrs. Margaret Washington put it, to those of the "lower" classes. Washington also referred to the women of the movement as New Negro Women long before the term was used by Alain Locke. Washington was a leader in the Black Club Women's Movement, and, as a Brittney Cooper has pointed out, the movement was at the forefront of advancing respectability politics. They felt that there was pressure to prove that they, too, were ladies. According to Paula Giddings, "In part, the proliferation of Black ladies' literary, intelligence, temperance, and moral improvement societies in this period was a reaction to that pressure."[8] Therefore, developing a race of people who live within the expectations of respectability, as Tempy sees it, means that class mixing was unacceptable for immorality is associated with the Black poor.

This is especially true of Black teenagers whom Tempy sees as lingering on the edge of sexual corruption. Teenaged girls' bodies are vessels for this kind of indecency. A young girl has the potential to lead her nephew morally astray and Tempy must restrict any contact with the forbidden. Instruction on morality comes not only with a fair number of restrictions but also with "a book written for young men on the subject of love and living, called *Doors of Life*, addressed to all Christian youths in their teens—but it had been written by a white New England minister of the Presbyterian faith who stood aghast before the flesh."[9] Common among the parenting is telling children what to avoid, which includes the practice of "how not to love" and to "beware of lewd women."[10] What to do was not a topic for discussion. Though it may be understandable why Tempy does not want Sandy to spend time with a classmate alone in her house, her reasons have more to do with the girl's class status and Tempy's fear of sex. This "casting down of eyes" approach, as W.E.B. Du Bois referred to it, is questioned by Sandy, who feels forced to sneak around and, eventually, to leave the house to live with his mother in Chicago. Tempy's unacknowledged fears leave him even more vulnerable to engaging in the activity that she tries to discourage. There is no open communication in the house he lives in that gives him an opportunity to ask questions and receive an answer that will help him to navigate the world of his adolescent peers. Further, there is no room for creativity. In other words, who is he? Ultimately, Sandy's inability to identify Tempy's fear of sex leads to a suppression of individual pursuits and longing to investigate the forbidden.

By the time he goes to Tempy's, he has already been exposed to Black folks' ways of indulging pleasure. As noted by Jason Miller, "In the novel, the blues itself seems to be a character, and Hughes worked to unify and blur traditional boundaries between the blues and gospel."[11] Blues music and accompanying performances challenge sexual suppression. Just as Sandy's relationship with his grandmother and mother are inspired by Hughes's biography, so is Jimboy's "blues education" and limited ideal of the South, which is based on Hughes's travels to southern black communities where he earned a "blues education in New Orleans."[12] According to Hughes, he takes a room on Rampart Street, "the leading Negro Street."[13] On Saturday nights, the second floor of the boarding house "was very gay," and there Hughes listened to "blues records on an old Victrola: Blind Lemon Jefferson, Lonnie Johnson, and Ma Rainey. And sometimes a wild guitar player would come in off the street and pluck a while, providing somebody bought him a drink or two. In Baton Rouge and New Orleans I heard many of the blues verses I used later in my short stories and my novel."[14]

Hughes's travels provided him with the opportunity not only to engage in poor southern Black communities but, more importantly, to see and feel the impact of "a wild guitar player" like Jimboy. In a conversation with his dad, Hughes tells him that he loves Negroes, "they have fun." Angela Davis notes, "few writers—with the exception of Langston Hughes, who often found himself at odds with his contemporaries—were willing to consider seriously the contribution blues performers made to black cultural politics."[15] "Fun" was an idea that his father, who had moved to Mexico because of racial discrimination in the United States, rejected for it would not pay the bills. As a result, Hughes would resent anyone he perceived as excising cultural expressions that he associated with the Black poor. Hughes promoted celebration of "the low-down folks, the so-called common element."[16] For Hughes, it was within those communities that Black culture was preserved. "Fun," for Black folks, is more than what it appears. When Jimboy is present, his purpose seems to provide the blues track to the family's life of struggle; his music and insight leads those who are willing to follow him to an escape from the miserable aspects on Black life and to tap into the interior or the souls of Black folks. In doing so, he gives them a glimmer of hope in a space that only requires them to be the self they are encouraged not to be by a respectable society.

Hughes uses Harriet to show what happens when a Black girl is confined and, realizing this, resists constraint to seize liberation. Having no other means to define her self, she uses the fullness of her body to achieve a level of freedom. Davis helps us to understand the significance of Hughes's blues woman. She states, "In the contemporary period, which is marked by a popular recognition of the politicization of sexuality, the blues constitute an exceptionally rich site for feminist investigation. The overarching sexual themes that define the content of the blues form point the way toward a consideration of the historical politics of Black sexuality. Considering the stringent taboos on the representations of sexuality that characterized most dominant discourses of the time, the blues constitute a privileged discursive site."[17] In other words, the blues give Harriet a voice (literally and figuratively) before she has a voice, in her home or in the society that placed restrictions on her form of expression as a young Black woman. For Hughes, the blues and Black people who indulge it in song and play give themselves permission to escape and have "fun." It is a time of laughter, when family or community can bond together in their love of Black expression, art, and performance. It is a time when the crimes of racism, such as lynching, Jim Crow segregation, low pay for hard work, and racially motivated disrespect, are laid down to focus on the Black self. A blues performance can empower the performer by placing the individual in a position to give voice to the masses as well as provide income. It is a form of pleasure-taking as well as pleasure-giving in which the performer and the observer participate in a mutual experience and share in the benefits of the experience.

Having limited resources, Harriet goes through risky changes in her efforts to have a career on stage. For Harriet, pursuing a career in this area is her attempt to have a life of pleasure and to deny respectability in a way that Hughes perceives it. Harriet's resistance to her mother as expressed by her refusal to attend church and to work for Whites presents as a denial of respectability, which is for Hughes a form of performing whiteness. About Whites, Harriet is able to state her position: "Darkies do like the church too much, but white folks don't care nothing about it at all. They're too busy getting theirs out of this world. Not from God. And I don't blame 'em, except that they're so mean to niggers. They're right though, looking out for themselves . . . and yet I hate 'em for it."[18] Harriet developed her philosophy about White folks by experience. Telling her story of shame and humiliation is an act of testifying and shows the connection between the church life she rejects and the blues life she will embrace. Testifying is a moment of public reflection as it acknowledges an event that caused the speaker to transition into a new phase of life. For Harriet, the moment of awareness occurs in the presence of her White peers in the Kansas school. Her classmates' decision to sit silently as she was removed from the section of the theater where she was seated with the class and told to move to one of the last three rows reserved for "colored" was shockingly revealing. Harriet recalls rising and "then stumbling up the dark aisle and out into the sunlight, her slender body hot with embarrassment and rage."[19]

Hughes's focus on a dark body that seeks the sunlight represents a two-step moment of transformation that begins with self-awareness and ends with resistance to what is known. This is an intensely personal moment. Rather than to comply with the "house rules" or societal expectations, she left the building equipped with the knowledge that Whites "would not have a single one of us around if they could help it."[20] That one moment of reality freed her to make decisions that focus on her self, a move toward embracing pleasure.

Harriet begins early to understand that there is a relationship between blues performance and her social status. Jimboy provides the tools for her escape through cultural performative practices when she is just a child. In defiance of her mother's protestations he and Harriet would sing together in the evenings. When they started, Harriet was a "little girl with braided hair."[21] Fully aware of his influence on her, her "roving brother-in-law . . . would amuse himself by teaching her the old Southern songs, the popular ragtime ditties, the hundreds of varying verses of the blues that he would pick up in the big dirty cities of the South."[22] Cheryl Wall takes note of the importance of these lessons, "He teaches her the full range of the rural blues man's repertoire: traditional folk seculars and ballads, popular ragtime tunes, and the floating lines of the blues."[23] Wall observes further, "Jimboy is also Harriet's dance instructor; he teaches her the parse me la, the buck and wing, and fundamentals of tap."[24] Ultimately, he helps her to access the whole being of her body, which she will then use to move far beyond her mother's yard.

At minimum, for Jimboy, his was a form of amusement, his own experience with pleasure that was made possible by his lifestyle. The bluesman complains of his inability to keep a steady job, prompting him to leave his wife and son to fend for themselves. As far as Aunt Hagar is concerned, besides fathering her grandson, his only acceptable contribution to the family is his ability to entertain. And, surely, entertainment through the blues and old southern songs as sung by these Black folks was a form of resistance to racial oppression in the South and its history of racial oppression. Hughes suggests that while still in braids, Harriet, like Jimboy, is a keeper of the blues tradition for her self first and for others second.

Harriet's musical mentor's claim of freedom would prove easier for him to exercise than it would for her. Indeed, he is a man and takes freedom at the expense of women who provide him with a home when he returns. In addition to physical freedom, Jimboy represented sexual freedom—a masculine privilege that he claimed without an apology or afterthought, but not to his wife whom he left behind with the child they conceived before they were married. Hughes uses language that makes this text into a highly sexualized one. In chapter V, the one chapter that prominently features a present Jimboy, Hughes carefully nods to Jimboy and Annjee as a sexually compatible couple: "Jimboy was home. All the neighborhood could hear his rich low baritone voice giving birth to the blues. On Saturday night he and Annjee went to bed early."[25] Later, the men of the community will talk about Harriet, known also as Harrie, in Sandy's presence. Whether Sandy is aware of the gendered double standard is not clear, but it is his observations of Harriet that pique his sexual curiosity.

While leaving and returning is possible for Jimboy, it would prove a major challenge for Harriet, as a Black woman's body is seen as belonging to the community and her family, but not to her self. Her choices, to be sure, would either hurt the race or uplift it. If Harriet's body will advance the race or the family, she makes clear that she will make every effort to use her dark body as she pleases. Just as Aunt Hagar represents the generation of old who believes that White people need Black folks to get by and living by respectable, Christian standards is the best way to survive, then Harriet is the generation of defiance who resists that way of being. As such, she is unwilling to follow her mother's rules and looks for compromises. While choosing the blues was an act of defiance— her choice would also extend to the spaces she would come to occupy and the amount of time she would spend in those spaces.

More specifically, Harriet's movements, even for short distances, have the potential to disrupt the hope of her mother's generation. Her decision to go with her boyfriend to the blues party, and to dance, for instance, is not merely a teenager's act of rebellion. It is there that readers learn just how dedicated she is to the culture of music and dance. Harriet all but disappears in the dance hall as soon as they enter: "the crowd moved like jelly-fish dancing on individual sea-shells, with Mingo and Harriet somewhere among the shakers. But they were not of them, since each couple shook in a world of its own."[26] Sandy enters Harriet's world, the place where she can embody her body like the other Black folks in the room and enjoy the pleasures of life while escaping the reality of being poor. Surely many of them are lost in the rhythm and promises of the blues music performed by the band and others are trying to find yet another self in a place that does not remind them of societal restrictions on their movements. In the dance hall, they can move as they will with the consent of another.

Drawing readers into Harriet's blues world means that we are given a snapshot of a visual, moving picture. A man who saw blues clubs as a classroom and wrote music lyrics and plays, Hughes clearly delves into his creative aspirations to capture the performance and feeling of the blues as Sandy sees it for the first time outside of the backyard performances. Indeed, what Sandy sees here is both communal for the people who have gone there to enjoy socializing with others and private for those who are seeking a connection with the emotions resonating from the music such as St. Louis Blues. Originally arranged and recorded by W. C. Handy, the song plays "with a burst of hopeless sadness."[27] Sandy observes the movement with a child's curiosity; he "opened his eyes to the drowsy flow of sound, long enough to pull together" and listens to the singer.[28] Interchangeably, as occurs between the cornet, banjo, and drums, Hughes describes the sound of the music and then gives the lyrics.

> St Louis woman with her diamond rings . . .
> . . . as the band said very weary things in a loud and brassy manner and the dancers moved in a dream that seems to have forgotten itself: Got ma man tied to her apron-strings . . . [29]

This is a shared moment of pleasure that takes the participants away from whatever worries bring them to the place where they can push back or resist hopelessness. The music does not ask them to forget, it seems to ask them to give into the experience of the truth of their circumstances—its loudness, its sadness, its hopelessness—and to move with the flow of it. In pleasure, there is no power struggle. Power becomes nonexistent, consumed. This is not to say that the person who has laid aside herself to pleasure is not empowered by the experience, but the giving in certainly is a part of the fulfillment of pleasure.

Sandy is introduced to this freedom, an experience that leads him to sexual desire and its intersection with women. As a child, he is not supposed to be there anymore than his aunt. Through his eyes, we learn the complexity of the space that he navigates and the fears of sex that ironically are present in a place where sex is ever present on the minds of the people on the dance floor. "Shame on you" is what he is told when he shares a piece of a fish sandwich with a girl he does not know. The mark of shame occurs in this narrative when it comes to even the possibility of male and female and even male and male sexual interactions. Following this incident, Sandy goes into the bathroom "smelling fishy" where men were "making fleshy remarks about the women they had danced with."[30] "Boy you out to try Velma" is the more specific comment that Sandy recalls hearing one of the young men say.[31] The smell, location, and banter cast a shadow on women as undesirable or bad. Why, he does not know, and neither do the men for they are merely acting out a social script that teases the unknown, silenced, and forbidden. From the dance floor to the men's room, Sandy is surrounded by sexual innuendo that makes a possible interaction between a hungry boy and girl a moment of pause. Unfortunately, the boy's lack of instruction from snatches of conversation in smelly places among strange young men, tauntings from peers, and grinding on the dance floor leaves him to fear girls.

Presumably, Harriet would have learned about her body and what she is not to do with it in a similar way. What we know for sure is that she is often told of the restrictions, but the reason for them are not shared in her mother's lists of nots. To restrict the body further, her mother will perform the patriarchal act of punishment through whipping—an act that Sandy will observe and receive reinforcement that there just may be something wrong with Black girls and women.

Punishment for explorations of the body and its sensual feelings is common in the novel. Sandy's observations of the women's lives are acts of voyeurism that place him as an observer—participate in punishment. Therefore, surely it becomes difficult to separate pleasure from pain. His ability to observe intimate moments—their suffering, their expressions of desire, their attempts to survive—mute his own sexual desires and heighten his sexual curiosities. The boy recalls in the chapter immediately following the "Dance," that after "Benbow's dance a few weeks ago . . . his Aunt Harriet had stood sullenly the next morning while Hagar whipped her—and hadn't cried at all, until the welts came under her silk stockings."[32] Interestingly enough, she is wearing silk stockings during the whipping. It would seem that her reaction was connected to the silk stockings, a material possession that to a maturing teenager could represent her budding sexual identity. If so, there is a suggestion that Aunt Hagar seeks to destroy the thing her youngest daughter cherishes as her own. The women and their interaction with each other and their community become a prism by which he sees their world and considers his role in it.

Further, within his memory of this moment where his aunt is punished for her night of pleasure and including him in that decision is his own fear of a sexual identity that is counter to the normative standards. In the next sentence, he lies in bed and thinks of Jimmy Lane who was forced to "wear his mother's shoes like a girl," a sentence that appears in the chapter titled "Punishment."[33] Sandy would later have to wear his mother's shoes when she too became too sick to work and buy him what he needed. Such sexual repression is prominent in the novel and seems to haunt Sandy. As with the shoes, his fear that he will be considered a girl is most certainly a form of punishment for his sexual curiosity, and, quite possibly, homoerotic feelings. Sandy continues to observe his aunt as she remains determined to define her own path.

Seeking her independence from her mother and what she represents, Harriet begins her career as a public performer. Only Sandy knows this. Leaving his father's side to explore the town's carnival with his friend leads him into the forbidden. There he observes his aunt dancing to the men's delight. He sees a "a bald-headed Negro . . . beating out a rag," "a white man . . . watching a slim black girl, with skirts held high and head thrown back, prancing in a mad circle of crazy steps."[34] After the performance, she goes where he cannot see her with the piano player and the White man, forcing readers to consider the Black woman's occupation of a private place where she must give of herself to make something of her self and for her self. What she gets out of the performance is limited to Sandy's childish perspective, but it is certainly her opportunity to further affirm her independence from her mother, who is at the same moment taking part in a church revival. The carnival is thought to be a place for heathens to indulge in pleasures that are antithetical to the work of praising God. It was also a place where many blues performers established their careers. Carnival revelers' pleasure defies the standards of respectability. She would soon pack her suitcases and leave her mother's home to travel with the carnival. Harriet is modeled after the many Black women performers who honed their craft with vaudeville, circuses, or carnivals. More specifically, Cheryl Wall sees the influences of blues women's biographies on Hughes's construction of Harriet. According to Wall and various biographers, Bessie Smith, whom Hughes would befriend, "began her career as a professional in a traveling show in 1912 when she was eighteen, she had been singing for nickels and dimes in her hometown of Chattanooga since age nine."[35] Memphis Minnie, whom Hughes wrote of later, did the same.

Poor but optimistic, Harriet's pursuit of pleasure orders her steps, so to speak. Her return to Stanton and her move to the Bottoms illuminates her transition from wistful girl to a blues subject. She becomes the woman her mother fears she will become. Sandy learns from the banter of men and seeing his aunt walking around town that she is involved in something worth talking about. Whether he ever actually learns that she is a prostitute has much to do with Hughes keeping him as a naive child whose ignorance is due to his grandmother's protection and later his respectable and Aunt Tempy's fear that knowledge comes from experience. Yet, his time working in the barbershop exposes him to the fact that Harrie, as the men refer to her, is a favorite among them. Harriet's refusal to move back into her mother's home, but to make sure that her nephew knows how to contact her in case of an emergency, demonstrates that what she keeps to herself is the choice of her body, but it is not her intent to sever ties with her family.

Her final departure from Stanton to become the performer that she seeks to be gives her an opportunity to use her body as she chooses and to define her self. Not until the end of the novel does Hughes give the reader an opportunity to see Harriet as an individual. Prior to his description of her on the stage we have seen her perform as part of a family gathering and referenced as one of the dancers in the blues hall. On this night, Hughes is careful to lead us to the spotlight that features Harriet in a moment of public pleasure. Hughes draws our attention to the stage by announcing her entrance, "'This is Harriet's part now,' Sandy whispered" to his mother.[36] Following this statement "the floodlights were lowered and the spotlight flared."[37] Throughout the narrative, Hughes gives meticulous detail about what Harriet is wearing at a given time. It is usually her clothing that signals to her mother that she is going somewhere to do something of which Aunt Hagar finds morally reprehensible. For the first time in the novel, she is shown as a woman who, among the Chicago "Black Belt audience," is accepted for who she is.[38] As a character of transition, she is able to show the connection between the past and the present. Her first song is "a new song—a popular version of an old Negro melody, refashioned with words from Broadway."[39] Hughes uses language that attempts to both celebrate her as a woman of African descent as it marks her as a woman who is of African descent. The speculative narrator states, "Harriet entered in a dress of glowing orange, flame-like against the ebony of her skin, barbaric, yet beautiful as a jungle princess."[40] She is of "ebony skin" and "barbaric" but still beautiful. In effect, she is the African exotic that Hughes had described in other work, such as his poem "Danse Africaine" (1920), "Dance! / A night-veiled girl / Whirls softly into a / Circle of light."[41] To emphasize her beauty, Sandy exclaims, "Gee, Aunt Harrie's prettier than ever!"[42]

Through the boy's eyes, Harriet has undergone a transformation that shows her as a woman who has come from her mother's house in Stanton to a woman in command of her self, her body, and her art. Her final act accentuates her performance as a practice of pleasure, where she is simultaneously on the stage stirring the emotions of her audience while maintaining a private space. Sandy seems to understand that his sight is limited: "On the stage the singer went on—as though singing to herself—her voice sinking to a bitter moan as the listeners rocked and swayed."[43] Harriet is there, but not there. Through her voice, she gives the audience an opportunity to channel their own feelings and emotions about the "blue mornin' when yo' daddy leaves yo' bed."[44] Ultimately, as Wall asserts, Harriet's triumph is her "successful invention of a life which she can lead without denying herself."[45]

Harriet contrasts painfully with Annjee as evidenced when she does not confirm Sandy's observation about his aunt's beauty and skills, twice. Instead she says, "Same old Harriet. But kinder horse." Persistent in his belief he "cries," "Sings good, though." Just as persistent in hers, Annjee rebuffs her son: "'She's the same Harrie,' murmured Annjee."[46] Her sentiment expresses a stance that Harriet has not risen above her circumstances to achieve any level of greatness that Annjee is willing to acknowledge. Annjee, who has not risen past her circumstances, as I will discuss later, may be unable as much as unwilling to see her sister in the present. Her sister's successful attempts to become the Black woman that does not fit the description of the woman her mother wanted her to be has been realized. As such, occupying a space of the future rather than living in the past is what is most prominent in her performance. She both acknowledges where she has come from as she speaks to where she is and where she hopes to be. Her songs remind

Sandy of "when papa used to play for her."[47] This slight reference is a dismissal of Jimboy who disappeared into the war (maybe) but inspired the opportunity for Harriet to occupy the space he left vacant.

Her pursuit of pleasure in resistance to respectability proves worth the strain it had on her and her mother's relationship. Upon Sandy's move to live with his mother—a woman who clearly only wants her son near to help her pay bills and to keep her company in her husband's absence—it is Harriet who encourages the boy to finish school. Hagar and Tempy's hope is that Sandy would study and position himself to uplift the race has not been forgotten by the teenager. Although he is willing to work, his mother's insistence that he work full-time to care of himself and to help her is not a goal he is willing to pursue nor is it fair. Harriet reenters their lives in time to criticize her sister's self-centeredness and to promise to pay for the boy's fees. Sandy's hope to remain in school and not to continue to work as an elevator operator is motivated by his plan to not get stuck in that position with no education and no chance of other options like the older men on the job. There is a lesson that Black men cannot advance without Black women and that Black women cannot advance without Black men. For this family, Jimboy's encouragement of Harriet when she was a child to develop her gift as a singer and dancer gave her the means to support her nephew's pursuit of his own pleasure. Harriet's success and plans to advance further in her career also show that a Black woman's pursuit of pleasure does not mean the race suffers but that it could advance, at least according to Hughes.

Although her character is not as developed as Harriet's, Annjee pursues pleasure as well. For Hughes, her pursuit places her in the position of failing as a mother. Annjee's greatest flaw is that, unlike her sister, her happiness in life is depended on the presence of her husband. Although for the most part readers are limited to what Sandy sees and hears, the narrative shifts perspectives to give insight into the woman Sandy could never know. As she laments over Jimboy's absence, she thinks he, "loved her, Annjee was sure of that. And it was not another woman that made him go away so often."[48] Rather, as far as Annjee could reason, it is that "he was born running, he said, and had run ever since."[49] In fact, it is his willingness to move from one place to the other that Annjee finds most attractive. Although she confesses that the reason they married was due to her pregnancy, what brought them together was her deeply rooted desire to leave Stanton. Only her traveling husband can promise that. By shifting narrative viewpoints, Hughes suggests that a son cannot understand the interior motivations of his mother. Hers is a private longing that no one can understand, but the man she longs for. Sex with Jimboy forces her to think she can leave her mother's home. After thinking how "glad" she'll be when he returns, she makes a promise that she only shares later with her mother, to follow him. In words that reveal a level of sincere anguish: "But if he goes off again, I'll feel like dying in this dead old town. I ain't never been away from here nohow."[50] Annjee has her own blues song. Without them knowing it, both Harriet and Annjee have been inspired by the whims of a traveling blues man to leave Stanton. They also have one other thing in common: a mother who believes they should stay and work. Realizing this, Annjee justifies her plan to leave her son behind by saying that she will send money back and that her sister Harriet can stay home with their mother. Her leaving, Annjee reasons, will keep her sister from "runnin' the streets so much."[51]

Pursuing pleasure for the self may have consequences. Annjee's problem is not her desire but her lack of acknowledging that she and Jimboy have obligations as parents. Her dismissal of his tendency to leave her behind as early as a few days after their son was born may show his ability to exercise a kind of freedom that gives him access to a world far beyond her own, but his absence has an impact on the family. Any plan to follow him means, then, that she is also shirking her responsibility as a parent. Aunt Hagar's loyalty to her family may eclipse her daughters' plans for themselves, but their plans often leave them in perilous situations that leaves her, as their mother, powerless to rescue them. She is unable to send money to Harriet when she is abandoned by the show and she is unable to provide a Christmas gift for her grandson when

Annjee is too sick to work. Pleasure, Hughes shows, comes with a price that may mean sacrificing family obligations to focus on the self. Further, the pursuit of pleasure does not guarantee that what a woman seeks she will find or should find. Unlike Harriet, Annjee does not find more than what she leaves behind. Instead, she has more of the same: work a job that barely pays the bills.

Ultimately, Annjee's escape to Chicago means that she lives in a one-bedroom apartment in the South Side's Black Belt. There, she must call for the son she abandoned to help her to pay for the meager life she is now living in a northern city that has made promises of freedom it does not keep. Further, as was the case in Stanton, she is without Jimboy. It is not made known whether she has ever considered the fact that Jimboy has not asked her to come with him as he moves about. Though she may desire him, there is little evidence that he desires her. Annjee's failure to define what happiness means to her irrespective of being with a man who has never made himself available to her for longer than a couple of weeks leaves her vulnerable to misery. Her stark shift from a woman who tries to give her son a sled to make him happy when a boy to a woman who abandons him and then expects him to give up his own dream of education to take care of her shows her as a woman who is trapped in a cycle from which she cannot escape. Of the three sisters, there is little hope for Annjee to move beyond the stage of dreaming. However, by the end, when the reality of her life becomes clear, she has no place else to go.

If Aunt Hagar is reminiscent of Hughes's grandmother, then Annjee is certainly modeled after his mother, Carolina "Carrie" Mercer Langston, born in 1873 to Charles Langston and Mary Leary on a farm near Lawrence, Kansas. Her family was deeply dedicated to engaging artistic culture and participating in local politics. Considered "the Belle of Black Lawrence," Carrie became involved with her father's Inter-State Literary Society where she gave public readings and developed her interest in becoming an actress.[52] She would later marry and divorce James Hughes and leave their son Langston off and on in the care of her mother and later family friends after the death of her mother and her marriage to Homer Clark. Carrie followed Homer from city to city, leaving her son to live with others and finally alone. When Hughes was sixteen, Homer left Carrie for a job in Chicago and she joined him with her stepson, leaving Hughes alone in Cleveland where he finished high school. Following her on-again-off-again husband would take her to numerous cities, including New York; McKeesport, Pennsylvania; and Atlantic City, New Jersey. She died of breast cancer in 1938. Except for a small role in Hall Johnson's *Run, Little Chillun*, she never enjoyed the success in acting that she had hoped for. Instead, she relied heavily on her son for financial and emotional support.

Perhaps it is Carrie Clark's lack of satisfaction and unfulfilled desire for something—a need to feel loved, seen—that propelled Hughes's interest in the pleasure of Black women. Contained in the letters she writes to her son over the years is a strong sense of longing. Clark's father's death left the family financially unstable, a position from which she never recovered. With her high school diploma, it is clear from her letters that she managed to work many kinds of jobs, including those as a "schoolteacher, stenographer, and domestic."[53] Clark made her only son responsible for the happiness that she could not attain on her own as she indulged the "wanderlust" of Homer Clark.[54] Surely his constant movement in search of employment was emotionally challenging to the woman who was left not only to fend for herself in whatever city he had left her but also to care for *his* son, Gwyn. Whatever frustration she felt was transferred to the son she had left behind. Sandy's pressure to leave or go to live with his mother is from the pages of Hughes's biography, as scholars have noted, "Her requests evolved into demands, as when, in his senior year of high school, she engaged him in a tug of war between school and work. For Carrie, Langston's potential as a laborer and contributor to her financial well-being was infinitely more valuable than his education."[55] Yet, although Annjee is selfish and self-centered in her actions, Hughes's literary version of himself, Sandy, is excited to leave home, thus giving him an opportunity to have a pleasurable experience until, of course, the reality of having to choose between work and education sets in.

Clark's letters to her son reflect her anguish as she tried to find a place in the lives of men and in society. This emotional conundrum remained at the heart of his relationship with his mother. In their assessment of the letters, Carmeletta M. Williams and John Edgar Tidwell see "her entreaties for money as tests of his love for her."[56] He would be expected, in many ways, to do the work that her father failed to do because of his death and both her husbands failed to do because of James Hughes's and Homer Clark's moves. Hughes was the one man she hoped to rely on to provide more than perhaps a mother should expect from a son to whom she gave so little. In her lack of understanding her son, readers might find empathy, for it is clear that the woman is lonely, and at times, in dire need financially. Just as it was not unusual for her to ask him for money or to at least hint that she needed some to help pay for rent, purchase a coat, shoes, and so on, it was not unusual for her to ask him to visit or to please write to her. Money was her emotional salve. In a letter she wrote in 1926, she opened, "Oh! I wish I could see you tonight. I am lonely. Oh! So lonesome to see you. It seems that I am getting old and I have never seen you very much." She ends, "Write me I am not so lonesome."[57] To be sure, this letter ignores the fact that they were apart as a result of the choices *she made* to leave her son with others until she abandoned him. During the course of the letter, she also described her time with Gwyn that involved playing the gramophone and listening to and singing Clara Smith's blues songs. Hughes may have felt the sting of the good times his mother described having with her stepson as much as he may have felt her loneliness and her need to be loved. With his mother, there could be no simplicity. One emotion was bound to another.

Beyond her attempts to remain connected to her son is her influence on his writing and love for the arts. As Williams and Tidwell observe, "In nearly all the attention devoted to Hughes's blues and jazz ethos. Humor. Vernacular voicings, and poetic innovations, the possible role Carrie may have played in her son's vast array of stylistic experiments and literary production has been nearly ignored."[58] Clark loved being the mother of Langston

Hughes. She clearly took deep pleasure in it and saw herself as an extension of his success. She wrote to him often about reading reviews of his work and the people who asked when he would visit. She also seemed to know some of the "celebrities" of the Harlem Renaissance and saw her acquaintances with them as a way to connect with her son. She made several references to Zora Neale Hurston, at one point saying that Hurston asked her to come to live with her. These letters are almost always a form of sharing something of the self, an opportunity to reveal something to the reader, but as revealing as they are, the intent is consistently hidden from the reader as well. As much as Clark may have relished the increasing success of her son, her pleadings to him to come and see her, wherever she was and she was always moving from one month to the next, she also wanted from him a dependency that Hughes was unwilling to give into fully. If she was to attain happiness, she could not rely on him to provide it.

For a moment, Clark attained pleasure in the work she was doing as an actress in a play. She wrote to Hughes from New York on February 15, 1933: "I am one of the principals in Hall Johnson's show 'Run Little Chillun Run.' Hall himself wrote this show and it is a discussion between two churches or rather the Hope Baptist Church of Charlestown."[59] A play about "the conflict between the Christian and African religious heritage in Black life," it reflected the feeling of religion that is represented through private performance. She was proud to report, "The critics are very enthusiastic about it and say they believe the play will last a year here."[60] Lack of pay caused a disruption, but more funding gave her an opportunity to return to the show in Pennsylvania. She left behind Gwyn and reported that, "We opened last night with a wonderful house."[61] Clark's pleasure is realized in the accomplishment of being able to act on stage. Acting presented her with an escape from her misery that involved constant relocating to new cities in search of employment, which proved especially difficult during the Great Depression of the 1930s. Her son's continued success despite the economic crisis sustained her shortfalls, but it could not give her the satisfaction she desperately sought. Ultimately, Clark wanted to be seen and acknowledged. Her desires were personal, but they required the public's support. Someone must recognize her as capable of delivering lines effectively and someone must pay her for her efforts. This someone must be a man, for the society in which she lived was (and still is) dominated by men's influences. But the goal is hers and to have a few weeks in the "principal role" gave her something that was hers, finally.

Inspired by the struggles of his own life, Hughes's voyeuristic perspective on Black women and pleasure through the fictional lens of a boy is speculative. Illuminating the desires of Black women to define themselves and their happiness was something that Hughes worked to achieve in *Not Without Laughter*. His relationship with his mother and grandmother clearly inspired his celebration and critique of Black women and sexuality. Within the freedom of expression, Hughes saw Black women who dared to defy respectable expectations to define their idea of what a Black woman could be or wanted to be, and through them, we see the costs and joys of pursuing pleasure.

Conclusion

Black Feminist Musings from Nature—The Context of Pleasure in 2020

Pleasure is a privilege. This is the lesson I learned during the first year of the COVID-19 pandemic. It is a time when there is to be no touching, no physical socializing. We have been told by doctors during the daily coverage of the pandemic, which began as a few cases in the United States as early as January 2020, that we can stop the spread of the virus if we stay six feet apart. Later we learn that more distance is needed to avoid minute droplets that can spew from our mouths when we sneeze, cough, or even talk. Pleasure is a privilege. Pleasure can also kill you.

Before North Carolina governor Roy Cooper announced that we would undergo a shelter-in-place mandate from March 20 until April 29, I had been home for a week and a half. Universities across the country had closed and we were preparing for online teaching. I wondered how I would hold on to myself during this time of isolation or, I should say, time of fear. This week, the week of April 6, which will end with Easter weekend, we are told this is to be the deadliest week yet. (Re)Defining pleasure may be essential to my survival.

I begin to rely on my senses to better understand what pleasure means to me. It never has been as important for me to possess this knowledge. On social media, many people confess to eating to fill the time. I do the same. Dealing with the fact that I have an amazing ability to begin cooking a desired meal only to learn that I do not have a key ingredient, I engage in unplanned experiments. I allow my tastes and desire for something good to guide me. On the day I plan to make a simple shrimp fettuccini, I remember much too late that I used all the fettuccini pasta back in November for a pre-Thanksgiving meal. I substitute elbow pasta. Experience tells me the most important taste is that of the shrimp. I do not have the vocabulary to describe my love of seafood. Growing up in the New Orleans area, I acquired a taste for seasoned seafood. I add garlic salt, onion powder, a bit of salt and pepper. Then I mix in sprinkles of Tony Chachere's Creole seasoning. I have purchased a bag of onions to aide with the sauté process. The aroma fills my kitchen. Stirring together a can of celery soup and mushroom soup, I savor the smell emanating from the pan and know that I am on the right track. I give the pan my full, undivided attention, which is why I don't prefer cooking most days. Cooking takes time, effort. Finally, the shrimp are almost tender enough and I turn off the heat and pour them into the mushroom and celery soup mixture that I poured over the substituted macaroni shells. I mix in more spices. This is the day's pleasure goal; when I am done, there will be enough for me to freeze and eat in weeks to come. This meal must be perfect. I close my eyes and taste. It's never good enough until I put in more effort, and, then, finally it is. A last step in my improvised casserole is to add the last bit of shredded cheese I find in my refrigerator to the top of the casserole before I place it in the oven. My need for indulgence helps me to forget that I have high cholesterol. Pleasure is a privilege for some. But it can also kill you.

On another day, I begin by making pancakes with a mix I bought at the store. It's gluten-free, so I am skeptical. I must make sure that I am not disappointed, for this is not the time for disappointments. I follow the directions to the letter, except I add a teaspoon of sugar and some cinnamon to the mix. This very important decision turns out to be the best one I'll probably make all day. After pouring the batter into my skillet, and making two,

I close my eyes and taste a piece of the finished products. They do not look like the ones on the package; mine are not round but oblong and ragged on the ends. But, I savor the flavor. It reveals to me a kind of softness that I find comforting. I am pleased.

Cooking and eating feeds the body, but what about my mind and spirit? I do not do well staying indoors. Some years ago I concluded that being able to go outside is a privilege of pleasure that I should not take for granted. Being related to several men who spent time in prison and reading prison narratives has made me conscious of the pleasure of freedom. Therefore, I go out with a purpose, even if it is only to the mailbox.

Every other day, during the shelter-in-place order, I enjoy the outdoors. Houses in my neighborhood are surrounded by trees of all kinds. It is April and most trees have bloomed. My nature journey begins inside. In the mornings, I walk into my bathroom and look at my neighbor's redbud from the window. I feel such happiness when I see the morning sun's rays shining upon the tree's pink flowers. It feels like an undeserved treat. As expected, the trees attract birds that sing and chirp in what seems like their attempt to infect the listeners with the pleasure of their gaiety.

From a wind chime that dangles from the roof of my front porch, I hear music that the former owner left behind. It is the perfect gift. I have never thought much about the wind as anything more than a nuisance, but the chime makes me consider how the wind communicates with us. I find myself drawn to a presence that begs me to be present. The chime itself looks old. It's made of a kind of metal and is attached by wood and sturdy string. If I saw it at a yard sale, I would not be impressed. But I have come to love the sound of it. I search for it especially at night when I hear no other noise but the music and an occasional owl.

In the afternoons, I no longer walk in the park. Too many people have taken to being there. Some stand in groups. Others walk straight past me and I find myself turning my head and stepping off the path. Only I seem concerned about my safety. Walking in the park is a privilege and a pleasure, maybe.

Instead, I begin to explore my neighborhood. Although my presence in a predominantly White neighborhood that was not built with me in mind captures attention, I refuse to be a prisoner in my own home. There is no pleasure in fear, but I take the chance that my brown body, with its relatively small frame, will not be criminalized, especially since some of these neighbors know my name. Armed with pepper spray, I do a speed walk every other day. Most afternoons I see very few people. One afternoon I hear voices, but do not see the sources of the voices. Suddenly, one neighbor hollers hello at me. I am startled by her friendliness, which disrupts the music I listen to through my earbuds. This day I'm walking to songs curated on the India.Arie station on Pandora. Neo-soul keeps me company in the bareness of the sunlit day. The music is set low so I can hear the music of nature. Many trees mean many birds. They chirp, sing. I wonder what they are saying. Do they know of the dangers we humans face? Squirrels dart out in front of me. I know they are jumping from tree to tree in the wooded area to my left. There, I hear dead pieces of wood and nuts hit the ground every now and again. The surrounding trees are a playground for the animals, I imagine. I round the corner and a red cardinal lands a few feet in front of me. I have seen many of them before on campus, but I am beginning to realize that they are closer to me than I knew. In the distance, I hear a lawn mower.

I fell in love with the neighborhood two years ago. The area where I live is not marked by a sign. You have to live here to know here. "You live in the woods," my colleague who grew up in this city tells me, after asking me how I found this place. We are sitting at my dinner table to enjoy a gathering of colleagues over a bowl of gumbo. I was called, I say to him. Each green lawn is accented with flowers, mostly azaleas. But there are other flowers whose names I do not know. Most of my yard had so much greenery I had some of it removed, but not enough that I cannot provide a space for the birds, squirrels, chipmunks, and bumblebees.

I bought this house in this neighborhood for the purpose of pleasure. Nature calls through multiple voices. Writing forces me to rely more on all of my senses to experience the world around me. On another evening, I walk and notice that most of the flowers in the neighborhood are varieties of pink, white, and red. I begin to wonder why. Every now and again I see wildflowers of purple and yellow. Purple ones have spread across my yard and my neighbors', which my neighbor complains about as he digs them out of his perfectly manicured lawn. These are weeds, he declares. I only see the color purple. My lawn folks leave some of them in my yard and I do not complain.

I take a different route on this humid day. According to the Weather app on my phone, it is 82 degrees outside, but it's cloudy. Bearable. As I charge forward, I notice for the first time that there is a direct route to one of the lakes on a street that is perpendicular to mine. I never noticed it before. Several weeks later I rush down the short path and discover that the swans I had read about live in a little lake. They are white and beautiful. Quiet. Observant. They have one another and we have them. I smile as I leave the path and turn on the next street. I hear birds singing, but the most obvious sound is that of a dog barking. Thankfully, I can't see it. But it is a dog that I (too) often hear breaking through the serenity of the neighborhood. I notice that the cars are layered in yellow dust, a clear indication that the pollen count is high. I search my senses to detect how my body is reacting to the air. I am thankful that my allergies are cooperating with my desire to breathe as my pace quickens. As I near the end of the street, I smell the sweetness of compost mixed with bark. Someone has spread it out in their front yard. I slow my pace a bit to take in the smell so thick I feel like it is touching me.

I see more people out today. A couple is walking a dog. The man glances back at me a few times. I begin to wonder why. I have no intention of getting close to them. We are at least forty feet apart and that is fine with me. At the corner, they go in a direction I plan to avoid. Walking farther, I hear voices. I notice that there are teenagers sitting together, but not really. They are spread out across a nicely manicured front lawn, socializing—from a distance. On the next street, a man jogs toward me. I cross the street.

He has seen me, but chooses not to acknowledge me. Invisibility will not protect us. Five minutes later, I am home.

During the walk, I have time to think more about the music I hear streaming through my earbuds. Beginning with India. Arie's "I Am Ready for Love," then Tamia's "There's a Stranger in My House," and lastly Jesse Powell's "You." These love songs are a kind of declaration of feelings and emotions set to music (melody, harmony) and a beat that remind me of another time. In the time of COVID-19, I notice that these songs have one thing in common: the singers project a kind of dependency on another or the hope of another or disappointment in another. Or, in other words, what one is or is not doing for the other. I don't find pleasure in dependency or in wishing for unfulfilled desire.

What I do find is that pleasure is defined by the context of a moment. I think I better understand Yolande, Lena, Minnie, and Moms, maybe even Carrie. These are women who used what they had to be who they were. From their stories, I begin to realize that pleasure is where I am. I have learned to find myself in the moment—to think carefully about how I am feeling and why I am feeling a certain way. In pleasure, I find a hidden self. And, I am pleased.

Acknowledgments

Many thanks for the enormous support I received from the Linda Carlisle Excellence Professorship, including the assistance of wonderful graduate students Chase Hanes, Danielle LaPlace, and Taylor Steadman. My colleagues of Women's, Gender, and Sexuality Studies (WGSS), including past director Mark Rifkin and current director Lisa Levenstein, have gone beyond expectations to support my research. Thanks also to Sarah Cervenak, Daniel Coleman, and Danielle Bouchard for the many conversations, suggestions, and extensions of support. And to Sheila Washington, the extraordinary former program coordinator of WGSS who made sure I was covered in a myriad of ways, thank you for all that you did to keep us going.

Thanks also for the generous support of Vanderbilt University's Callie House Research Center for the Study of Global Black Cultures and Politics and the invaluable advice and discussions provided by Black feminist scholars at our annual Fugitives writing retreats. Their advice gave me direction about how Black women define pleasure in ways that expanded my own thinking.

A book is not written without the inspiration of an idea that develops over time and during meaningful conversations with others. Thanks to Linda Carlisle, Tony Bolden, Willi Coleman, Danille K. Taylor, Stephanie Rook, Aries Powell, Barbara McDade Gordon (Florida Mom) and students in my literature and Black Women's Studies courses. For those fabulous Black feminist scholars who shared their research in conversation with mine, courtesy of Linda Carlisle Excellence Professorship funding, E. Patrick

Johnson, Andrea Williams, Sharon Holland, Jennifer Nash, and T. Sharpley-Whiting, I thank you for asking the questions that expand our knowledge about Black women's lives.

I also acknowledge the work of the wonderful editorial staff at Rutgers University Press, especially the incredibly patient editor Kim Guinta, who believed in this work and ushered it through the review process during a pandemic. Thanks also to the reviewers.

I acknowledge and remember the women of my family, my grandmothers Isabella and Lula who found pleasure in gardening and sharing their "fruits" with others. Thanks to my mother, father, and my family who taught me to love being my Black southern self, for their support, always.

Notes

Introduction

1. Hull, *Give Us Each Day*, 324.
2. Brooks-Higginbotham, "Black Church," 199.
3. Brooks-Higginbotham, 199.
4. Cooper, "Beyond Respectability," 19.
5. Lee, *Erotic Revolutionaries*, viii.
6. Collins, *Black Feminist Thought*, 74.
7. Collins, 81.
8. Mitchell, "Silences Broken," 436.
9. Mitchell, 436.
10. Stallings, 2.
11. Griffin, "Black Feminists and Du Bois," 34.
12. Oxford Lexico.com, s.v. "pleasure."
13. Nylan, "Lots of Pleasure," 1.
14. Nash, *Black Body in Ecstasy*, 3.
15. Bloom, *How Pleasure Works*, 24.
16. Green, "Interview with Kyrease Washington," *YouTube*.
17. brown, *Pleasure Activism*, 6.
18. brown, 15.
19. brown, 15.
20. Italics mine. Lorde, "Uses of the Erotic," 55.
21. Lorde, 57.
22. Lorde, 54–55.
23. Lorde, 56.

24. I provide a study of Alice Dunbar-Nelson's life and work or her pleasures in *Love, Activism, and the Respectable Life of Alice Dunbar-Nelson* (Bloomsbury, 2022).

25. Sharpley-Whiting, *Bricktops' Paris*, 12.

26. Sharpley-Whiting, 12.

27. Sharpley-Whiting, 41.

28. Sharpley-Whiting, 41.

29. Sharpley-Whiting, 6.

30. Chapman, *Prove It On Me*, 83.

31. Chapman, 83.

32. Bloom, *How Pleasure Works*, 141.

33. Morgan, "Why We Get Off," 37.

34. Morgan, 36.

35. Hartman, *Wayward Lives*, 28.

36. Hartman, 28.

37. Hartman, 221.

38. Hartman, 221.

39. Hartman, 17.

40. Hartman, 18.

41. Du Bois, "Criteria of Negro Art," para. 34.

42. Gates, "Why Richard Wright Hated Zora Neale Hurston," para. 1.

43. Gates, para. 1.

44. Tate, *Psychoanalysis and Black Novels*, 50.

45. Collins, *Black Sexual Politics*, 36.

46. Lindsey, *Colored No More*, 3.

47. Chapman, *Prove It On Me*, 15.

48. Locke, "New Negro," para. 4.

49. McDowell, *Changing Same*, 80.

50. McDowell, 79.

51. McDowell, 88.

52. Larsen, *Passing*, 189.

53. McDowell, *Changing Same*, 88.

54. Larsen, *Passing*, 148–149.

55. Larsen, 162.

56. Dean, "Gaze," 99.

57. Morgan, "Why We Get Off," 36.

58. Morgan, 36.

59. Collins, *Black Sexual Politics*, 51.

60. Morgan, "Why We Get Off," 37.

61. Hurston, "Characteristics," 50. Italics mine.

62. Hurston, 50.

63. Nash, *Black Body*, 3.

64. Collins, *Black Feminist Thought*, 10.

1. Finding Yolande Du Bois's Pleasure

1. Wall, *Worrying the Line*, 14.

2. Griffin, "Black Feminists and Du Bois," 29.

3. Griffin, 29.

4. Pauley, "W.E.B. Du Bois on Woman Suffrage," 135.

5. Lewis, *W.E.B. Du Bois*, 449.

6. Lewis, 451.

7. Lewis, 451.

8. Bolden, *Up close, W.E. B. Du Bois*, 124.

9. Lewis, *W.E.B. Du Bois*, 435.

10. Lewis, 435.

11. Bolden, *Up close, W.E.B. Du Bois*, 123.

12. Lewis, *W.E.B. Du Bois*, 435.

13. Cognard-Black and Walls, *Kindred Hands*, 3.

14. See W.E.B. Du Bois to Yolande Du Bois dated March 13, 1907. University of Massachusetts-Amherst Library.

15. Cognard-Black and Walls, *Kindred Hands*, 5.

16. See W.E.B. Du Bois to Yolande Du Bois dated March 13, 1907. University of Massachusetts-Amherst Library.

17. Griffin, "Black Feminists and Du Bois," 34.

18. Griffin, 35.

19. Du Bois wrote several letters to the principal of Brooklyn Girls' School expressing his outrage that the five senior graduates had not been invited to, were in fact prohibited from attending, the Senior Promenade.

20. See Yolande Du Bois to Nina Du Bois dated March 1921. University of Massachusetts-Amherst Library.

21. See Yolande to Nina Du Bois dated February 26, 1920. University of Massachusetts-Amherst Library.

22. See Yolande to Du Bois dated March 16, 1921. University of Massachusetts-Amherst Library.

23. Dyhouse, *Girl Trouble*, 5.

24. See Yolande to Cullen dated November 19, 1923. Beinecke Library. Yale University.

25. See Yolande to Cullen dated January 24, 1924. Beinecke Library. Yale University.

26. Lewis, *W.E.B. Du Bois*, 445.

27. Lewis, 445.

28. See Du Bois to Yolande dated August 29, 1923.

29. In an introductory letter, Du Bois wrote to the head of Bedales, the English school that he sent a teenaged Yolande to for a year; he ended by stating that he wanted his daughter to learn how to "walk on her own."

30. See Du Bois to Yolande dated August February 13, 1923. University of Massachusetts-Amherst Library

31. Ibid.

32. See Du Bois to Francis Hoggan dated March 10, 1925. University of Massachusetts-Amherst Library.

33. See Yolande Du Bois to Cullen dated May 10, 1926. Beinecke Library. Yale University.

34. See Yolande Du Bois to Cullen dated May 28, 1926. Beinecke Library. Yale University.

35. See Yolande Du Bois to Cullen dated May 10, 1926. Beinecke Library. Yale University.

36. See Yolande Du Bois to Cullen dated May 28, 1926. Beinecke Library. Yale University.

37. See Yolande Du Bois to Countee Cullen dated August 1926. Beinecke Library. Yale University.

38. "Countee Cullen to Marry Daughter of Dr. W.E.B. Du Bois, April 13, 1928."

39. See Du Bois to Yolande dated February 17, 1926. University of Massachusetts-Amherst Library.

40. Dyhouse, *Girl Trouble*, 8.

41. See Du Bois to Yolande dated January 13, 1928. University of Massachusetts-Amherst Library.

42. Ogbar, *Harlem Renaissance*, 55.

43. "Cullen-Du Bois Nuptials," January 28, 1928.

44. I am referring to a copy of a diary that is in the Countee Cullen Papers at the Amistad Research Center at Tulane University in New Orleans.

45. See Du Bois to Cullen dated September 11, 1928. Countee Cullen Papers. Amistad Center. Tulane University.

46. Ibid.

47. hooks, *Communion*, 77.

48. See Du Bois to Cullen dated September 18, 1928. Countee Cullen Papers. Amistad Center. Tulane University.

49. Nash, *Black Body in Ecstasy*, 150.

50. See Yolande Du Bois to Du Bois dated May 23, 1923. University of Massachusetts-Amherst Library.

51. "Cullen Suing for Divorce," February 28, 1929.

52. Lewis, *W.E.B. Du Bois*, 628.

53. hooks, *Communion*, xviii.

2. Lena Horne and Respectable Pleasure

1. Nash, *Black Body in Ecstasy*, 5.

2. Gavin, *Stormy Weather*, 10.

3. Horne, *Lena*, 9.

4. Horne, 9.

5. Horne, 9.

6. Horne, 9.

7. Gavin, *Stormy Weather*, 20.

8. Gavin, 20.

9. Gavin, 20.

10. Horne, *Lena*, 20.

11. Horne, 32.

12. Horne, 23.

13. Horne, 23.

14. Horne, 48–49.

15. Horne, 49.

16. Gavin, *Stormy Weather*, 33.

17. Gavin, 33.

18. Horne, *Lena*, 55.

19. Gavin, *Stormy Weather*, 44.

20. Horne, *Lena*, 50.

21. Gavin, *Stormy Weather*, 44.

22. Horne, *Lena*, 51.

23. Horne, 80.

24. Horne, 80.

25. Horne, 80.

26. Horne, 80.

27. Nash, *Black Body in Ecstasy*, 7.

28. Horne, *Lena*, 89.

29. Horne, 90.

30. Horne, 90.

31. Gavin, *Stormy Weather*, 66.

32. Gavin, 67.

33. Horne, *Lena*, 89.

34. Horne, 91.

35. Nash, *Black Body in Ecstasy*, 3.

36. Horne, *Lena*, 53.

37. Horne, 151.

38. Pullen, *Like a Natural Woman*, 109.

39. Dreher, *Dancing on the White Page*, 31.

40. Dreher, 33.

41. Pullen, *Like a Natural Woman*, 121.

42. Gavin, *Stormy Weather*, 132.

43. Gavin, 33.

44. Chapman, *Prove It On Me*, 129.

45. Gavin, *Stormy Weather*, 134.

46. Chapman, *Prove It On Me*, 129.

3. Moms Mabley and the Art of Pleasure

1. Thompson, "Picturing the Past."

2. Bennetts, "Theatre: The Pain beyond the Laughter of Moms Mabley," para. 9.

3. Williams, *Humor of Jackie Moms Mabley*, 41–42.

4. Williams, 42.

5. Sotiropoulos, *Staging Race*, 64.

6. Sotiropoulos, 65.

7. Petersen, *Profiles of African American Stage Performers*, 45.

8. Nelson, "Criminality and Sexual Morality," 271.

9. Monroe, "Courtship, Comedy, and African-American Expressive Culture," 180.

10. Butterbeans and Susie. "Oh Yeah!" *YouTube*, December 3, 2014, https://www.youtube.com/watch?v=1eA9CnSohgI.

11. Butterbeans and Susie, "Elevator Papa," lyrics.fandom.com.

12. Cullen, Hackman et al., *Vaudeville, Old and New*, 175.

13. Cullen, Hackman, 175.

14. Hurston, *Their Eyes Were Watching God*, 123.

15. Hurston, 111.

16. Hurston, *Mules and Men*, 2.

17. Wright, "Between Laughter and Tears," 17.

18. Wright, 17.

19. Gates, "Why Richard Wright Hated Zora Neale Hurston," para. 9.

20. Jones, *Critical Insights*, 67.

21. Hurston, *Mules and Men*, 3.

22. Hurston, 3.

23. Hurston, 37.

24. Hurston, 39.

25. Nassour, "Mom's Mabley," 334.

26. Hughes, *Big Sea*, 229.

27. Wilson, *Bulldaggers, Pansies, and Chocolate Babies*, 18.

28. Wilson, 45.

29. Wilson, 45.

30. Wilson, 44.

31. Hemenway, *Zora Neale Hurston*, 175–176.

32. Wilson, *Bulldaggers, Pansies, and Chocolate Babies*, 46.

33. Nassour, "Mom's Mabley," 334.

34. Carlin and Conwill, *Ain't Nothing Like the Real Thing Baby*, 12.

35. Bunch, "Foreword," 14.

36. Bunch, 15.

37. Bunch, 15.

38. Monroe, "Courtship, Comedy," 180.
39. Goldberg, *Whoopi Goldberg Presents.*
40. Welcome, "Our Bodies for Ourselves," 88.
41. Williams, *Humor of Jackie Moms Mabley*, 48.
42. Harry Belafonte assembled a cast of Black actors in 1967 to address Black identity. Mabley plays a Black couple's wise and witty maid that openly critiques their fear of being Black in their predominantly White neighborhood.
43. Tucker, *Furiously Funny*, 74.
44. Bunch, "Foreword," 17.
45. Tucker, *Furiously Funny*, 71.
46. Mabley, "Don't Sit on My Bed." *YouTube* video, 4:43, May 29, 2018, https://www.youtube.com/watch?v=4hot_teqE_E
47. Nassour, "Mom's Mabley," 343.
48. Williams, *Humor of Jackie Moms Mabley*, 49.
49. Tucker, *Furiously Funny*, 79.
50. "The Best of Moms Mabley and Pigment." *YouTube* video, 36:50, September 23, 2020, https://www.youtube.com/watch?v=YpJtdfQorKw.
51. Monroe, "Courtship, Comedy," 180.
52. "The Best of Moms Mabley and Pigment." *YouTube* video, 36:50, September 23, 2020, https://www.youtube.com/watch?v=YpJtdfQorKw.
53. Tucker, *Furiously Funny*, 76.
54. Tucker, 76.
55. "Moms Mabley - Live At Sing Sing." *YouTube* video, 1:05:29, September 25, 2016, https://www.youtube.com/watch?v=as9olj8QHIU.
56. Stallings, *Mutha Is Half a Word*, 4–5.
57. Williams, *Humor of Jackie Moms Mabley*, 53.
58. Cooper, *Beyond Respectability*, 94.
59. Nassour, "Mom's Mabley," 334.
60. Nelson, "Criminality and Sexual Morality," 266.
61. Wilson, *Bulldaggers, Pansies, and Chocolate Babies*, 14.
62. Russell, "Color of Discipline," 10.
63. Yancy, *Black Bodies, White Gazes*, 130.
64. Williams, *Humor of Jackie Moms Mabley*, 43.
65. "Mom's Mabley: Interview." *YouTube* video, 5:20, October 18, 2011, https://www.youtube.com/watch?v=PWW-96BouIU.

4. Memphis Minnie and Songs of Pleasure

1. De Santis, *Langston Hughes and the Chicago Defender*, 195.
2. Davis, *Blues Legacies*, xiii.
3. Garon and Garon, *Woman with a Guitar*, 15.
4. Garon and Garon, 14.
5. LaVere, "Memphis Minnie," 31.
6. LeVere, 31.
7. LeVere, 31.
8. McKee and Chisenhall, *Beale Black & Blue*, 15.
9. McKee and Chisenhall, 15.
10. McKee and Chisenhall, 15.
11. McKee and Chisenhall, 17.
12. Garon and Garon, *Woman with a Guitar*, 19.
13. Harrison, "Black Pearls," 10.
14. Davis, *Blues Legacies*, xv.
15. References to songs have been taken from *Complete Recorded Works, Vol. 2* and *When the Levee Breaks: The Best of Memphis Minnie*. Unless otherwise indicated, lyrics were transcribed by author.
16. McKee and Chisenhall, *Beale Black & Blue*, 126.
17. Davis, *Blues Legacies*, xvii.
18. Wasserman, "Queen Bee, King Bee," 11.
19. Garon and Garon, *Woman with a Guitar*, 105.
20. Garon and Garon, 107.
21. Garon and Garon, 108.
22. Garon and Garon, 108.
23. Garon and Garon, 110.
24. Garon and Garon, 108.
25. Tribbett, "Everybody Wants to Buy," 43.
26. Garon and Garon, *Women with a Guitar*, 47.
27. Stallings, *Mutha' Is Half a Word*, 3.
28. Garon and Garon, *Woman with a Guitar*, 61.
29. Chapman, *Prove It On Me*, 81.
30. Hartman, *Wayward Lives*, 61.
31. Davis, *Blues Legacies*, 3.
32. Garon and Garon, *Woman with a Guitar*, 160.

33. Garon and Garon, 69.

34. Garon and Garon, 69.

35. Garon and Garon, 50.

36. Garon and Garon, 68.

37. Tribbett, "Everybody Wants to Buy," 43.

38. Oakley, *Devil's Music*, 183.

39. Oakley, 183.

40. Garon and Garon, *Woman with a Guitar*, 70.

41. Garon and Garon, 70.

42. McKee and Chisenhall, *Beale Black & Blue*, 17.

43. Davis, *Blues Legacies*, 3.

44. Stallings, *Mutha' Is Half a Word*, 3.

5. Pleasurable Resistance in Langston Hughes's *Not Without Laughter*

1. Nylan, "Lots of Pleasure," 1.

2. Chapman, *Prove It On Me*, 10.

3. Weisenfeld, "Secret at the Root," 40.

4. Weisenfeld, 40.

5. Hughes, *Not Without Laughter*, 237.

6. Hughes, 237.

7. Hughes, 237.

8. Giddings, *When and Where I Enter*, 49.

9. Hughes, *Not Without Laughter*, 258.

10. Hughes, 258.

11. Miller, *Langston Hughes*, 47.

12. Hughes, *Big Sea*, 290.

13. Hughes, 290.

14. Hughes, 290.

15. Davis, *Blues Legacies*, xiii.

16. Hughes, "Negro Artist and the Racial Mountain," para. 4.

17. Davis, *Blues Legacies*, xvii.

18. Hughes, *Not Without Laughter*, 82.

19. Hughes, 82.

20. Hughes, 90.

21. Hughes, 63.

22. Hughes, 63.

23. Wall, *Worrying the Line*, 43.

24. Wall, 43.

25. Hughes, *Not Without Laughter*, 59.

26. Hughes, 95.

27. Hughes, 102.

28. Hughes, 102.

29. Hughes, 102.

30. Hughes, 98.

31. Hughes, 95.

32. Hughes, 119.

33. Hughes, 123.

34. Hughes, 113.

35. Hughes, 42.

36. Hughes, 292.

37. Hughes, 293.

38. Hughes, 291.

39. Hughes, 293.

40. Hughes, 293.

41. Hughes, "Danse Africaine," lines 6–8.

42. Hughes, "Danse Africaine," lines 6–8.

43. Hughes, *Not Without Laughter*, 294.

44. Hughes, 294.

45. Wall, *Worrying the Line*, 45.

46. Hughes, *Not Without Laugher*, 293.

47. Hughes, 294.

48. Hughes, 44.

49. Hughes, 46.

50. Hughes, 46.

51. Hughes, 46.

52. Williams and Tidwell, *My Dear Boy*, xxv.

53. Williams and Tidwell, 5.

54. Williams and Tidwell, 6.

55. Williams and Tidwell, 6.
56. Williams and Tidwell, 13.
57. Williams and Tidwell, 29.
58. Williams and Tidwell, 1.
59. Williams and Tidwell, 60.
60. Williams and Tidwell, 62.
61. Williams and Tidwell, 75.

Bibliography

Bennetts, Leslie. "Theater: The Pain Behind the Laughter of Moms Mabley." *New York Times.* August 9, 1987, A.5 (accessed August 10, 2021).

Bloom, Paul. *How Pleasure Works: Why We Like What We Like.* New York: W. W. Norton, 2010.

Bolden, Tonya. *Up Close, W.E.B. Du Bois: A Twentieth-Century Life.* New York: Viking, 2008.

Brooks-Higginbotham, Evelyn. "The Black Church, a Gender Perspective." In *African American Religious Thought: An Anthology*, edited by Cornel West and Eddie S. Glaude Jr. Louisville: Westminster John Knox Press, 2003.

brown, adrienne m. *Pleasure Activism: The Politics of Feeling Good.* Chico: AK Press, 2019.

Bunch, Lonnie. "Foreword." In *Ain't Nothing Like the Real Thing Baby: How the Apollo Theater Shaped American Entertainment*, edited by Richard Carlin and Kinshasha Holma Conwill. National Museum of African American History and Culture, 2010.

Butterbeans and Susie. "Oh Yeah! (1927)." *YouTube* video, 3:05. December 3, 2014. https://www.youtube.com/watch?v=1eA9CnSohgI.

Carlin, Richard, and Kinshasha Holma Conwill, eds. *Ain't Nothing Like the Real Thing Baby: How the Apollo Theater Shaped American Entertainment.* National Museum of African American History and Culture, 2010.

Chapman, Erin D. *Prove It On Me: New Negroes, Sex, and Popular Culture in the 1920s.* Oxford: Oxford University Press, 2012.

Cognard-Black, Jennifer, and Elizabeth Macleod Walls. *Kindred Hands: Letters on Writing by British and American Women Authors, 1865–1935.* Iowa City: University of Iowa Press, 2006.

Collins, Patricia Hill. *Black Feminist Thought: Knowledge, Consciousness, and the Politics of Empowerment*. New York: Routledge, 2000.

———. *Black Sexual Politics: African Americans, Gender, and the New Racism*. New York: Routledge, 2004.

Cooper, Brittney C. *Beyond Respectability: The Intellectual Thought of Race Women*. Urbana: University of Illinois Press, 2017.

"Countee Cullen to Marry Daughter of Dr. W.E.B. DuBois." *Interstate Tattler*. April 13, 1928. Infoweb (accessed June 1, 2019).

"Cullen-DuBois Nuptials." *New York Age*. January 28, 1928. Infoweb (accessed June 1, 2019).

Cullen, Countee. Letter from Countee Cullen to W.E.B. Du Bois, January 13, 1930. In *W.E.B. Du Bois Papers (MS 312)*. University of Massachusetts Amherst: Special Collections and University Archives.

Cullen, Frank, Florence Hackman, and Donald McNeilly. *Vaudeville, Old and New: An Encyclopedia of Variety Performers in America*. New York: Routledge, 2006.

"Cullen Suing for Divorce." *Philadelphia Tribune*. February 28, 1929.

Davis, Angela Y. *Blues Legacies and Black Feminism: Gertrude "Ma" Rainey, Bessie Smith and Billie Holiday*. New York: Penguin Random House, 1998.

Dean, Elizabeth. "The Gaze, the Glance, the Mirror: Queer Desire and Panoptic Discipline in Nella Larsen's Passing." *Women's Studies* 48, no. 2 (February 17, 2019): 97–103. https://doi.org/10.1080/00497878.2019.1580520.

De Santis, Christopher. *Langston Hughes and the Chicago Defender: Essays on Race, Politics, and Culture, 1942–62*. Urbana: University of Illinois Press, 1995.

Dreher, Kwakiutl L. *Dancing on the White Page: Black Women Entertainers Writing Autobiography*. Albany: State University of New York Press, 2008.

Du Bois, W.E.B. "Criteria of Negro Art." webdubois.org. Accessed February 10, 2021.

———. Letter from W.E.B. Du Bois to Yolande Du Bois, March 13, 1907. In *W.E.B. Du Bois Papers (MS 312)*. University of Massachusetts-Amherst Library. Special Collections and University Archives.

———. Letter from W.E.B. Du Bois to Yolande Du Bois, August 29, 1923. In *W.E.B. Du Bois Papers (MS 312)*. University of Massachusetts-Amherst Library: Special Collections and University Archives.

———. Letter from W.E.B. Du Bois to Yolande Du Bois, February 13, 1923. In *W.E.B. Du Bois Papers (MS 312)*. University of Massachusetts-Amherst Library: Special Collections and University Archives.

———. Letter from W.E.B. Du Bois to Francis Hogan, March 10, 1925. In *W.E.B. Du Bois Papers (MS 312)*. University of Massachusetts-Amherst Library. Special Collections and University Archives.

———. Letter from W.E.B. Du Bois to Yolande Du Bois, February 17, 1926. In *W.E.B. Du Bois Papers (MS 312)*. University of Massachusetts-Amherst Library: Special Collections and University Archives.

———. Letter from W.E.B. Du Bois to Yolande Du Bois, January 13, 1928. In *W.E.B. Du Bois Papers (MS 312)*. University of Massachusetts-Amherst Library. Special Collections and University Archives.

———. Letter from W.E.B. Du Bois to Countee Cullen, September 11, 1928. In *W.E.B. Du Bois Papers (MS 312)*. University of Massachusetts Amherst: Special Collections and University Archives.

———. Letter from W.E.B. Du Bois to Countee Cullen, September 18, 1928. In *W.E.B. Du Bois Papers (MS 312)*. University of Massachusetts Amherst: Special Collections and University Archives.

Du Bois, Yolande. Letter from Yolande Du Bois to Nina Du Bois, February 26, 1921. In *W.E.B. Du Bois Papers (MS 312)*. University of Massachusetts Amherst: Special Collections and University Archives.

———. Letter from Yolande Du Bois to Nina Du Bois, March 1921. In *W.E.B. Du Bois Papers (MS 312)*. University of Massachusetts Amherst: Special Collections and University Archives.

———. Letter from Yolande Du Bois to W.E. B. Du Bois, March 16, 1921. In *W.E.B. Du Bois Papers (MS 312)*. University of Massachusetts Amherst: Special Collections and University Archives.

———. Letter from Yolande Du Bois to Cullen, November 19, 1923. Countee Cullen Collection. Beinecke Library: Yale University.

———. Letter from Yolande Du Bois to Cullen, January 24, 1924. Countee Cullen Collection. Beinecke Library: Yale University.

———. Letter from Yolande Du Bois Cullen, May 10, 1926. Countee Cullen Collection. Beinecke Library: Yale University.

———. Letter from Yolande Du Bois Cullen, May 28, 1926. Countee Cullen Collection. Beinecke Library: Yale University.

————. Letter from Yolande Du Bois to Countee Cullen, August 1926. Countee Cullen Collection. Beinecke Library: Yale University.

————. Letter from Yolande Du Bois to Countee Cullen, May 23, 1929. Countee Cullen Collection. Beinecke Library: Yale University.

Dyhouse, Carol. *Girl Trouble: Panic and Progress in the History of Young Women*. London and New York: ProQuest Ebook Central, 2014.

Garon, Paul, and Beth Garon. *Woman with a Guitar: Memphis Minnie's Blues*. New York: De Capo Press, 1922.

Gates, Henry Louis, Jr. "Why Richard Wright Hated Zora Neale Hurston." The Root. Accessed March 18, 2013. https://www.theroot.com/why-richard-wright-hated-zora-neale-hurston-1790895606.

Gavin, James. *Stormy Weather: The Life of Lena Horne*. New York: Atria Paperback, 2009.

Giddings, Paula. *When and Where I Enter: The Impact of Black Women on Race and Sex in America*. New York: Bantam Books, 1985.

Goldberg, Whoopi. "Whoopi Goldberg Presents Moms Mabley." HBO, 2013.

Green, Tara T. "Interview with Kyrese Washington." *YouTube* video, 57:28. September 30, 2020. https://youtu.be/a5jmghRdI7s.

Griffin, Farah J. "Black Feminists and Du Bois: Respectability, Protection, and Beyond." *ANNALS of the American Academy of Political and Social Science* 568, no. 1 (March 2000): 28–40. https://doi.org/10.1177/0002716 20056800104.

Harrison, Daphne Duval. *Black Pearls Blues Queens of the 1920s*. New Brunswick, NJ: Rutgers University Press, 1988.

Hartman, Saidiya. *Wayward Lives, Beautiful Experiments: Intimate Histories of Social Upheaval*. New York: W. W. Norton & Company Inc., 2019.

Hemenway, Robert. *Zora Neale Hurston: A Literary Biography*. Urbana: University of Illinois, 1980.

hooks, bell. *Communion: The Female Search for Love*. New York: William Morrow, 2002.

Horne, Lena. *Lena*. New York: DoubleDay, 1965.

Hughes, Langston. *The Big Sea*. New York: Hill and Wang, 1993.

————. "Danse Africaine." Poetry Nook. Accessed February 10, 2020. https://www.poetrynook.com/poem/danse-africaine.

———. "The Negro Artist and the Racial Mountain." Poetry Foundation. Accessed February 10, 2020. https://www.poetryfoundation.org/articles /69395/the-negro-artist-and-the-racial-mountain.

———. *Not Without Laughter*. New York: Macmillan, 1969.

Hull, Gloria, ed. *Give Us Each Day: The Diary of Alice Dunbar Nelson*. New York: W. W. Norton & Co. Inc., 1986.

Hurston, Zora Neale. "Characteristics of Negro Expression." In *Folklore, Memoirs, and Other Writings*, edited by Cheryl A. Wall. New York: Library of America, 1995.

———. *Mules and Men*. New York: Harper Perennial, 1990.

———. *Their Eyes Were Watching God*. New York: HarperCollins, 1990.

Jones, Sharon L. *Critical Insights: Zora Neale Hurston*. Pasadena, CA: Salem Press, 2013.

Larsen, Nella. *Passing*. New York Penguin Books, 2020.

LaVere, Steve. "Memphis Minnie." Accessed February 10, 2021. https:// sundayblues.org.

Lee, Shayne. *Erotic Revolutionaries: Black Women, Sexuality, and Popular Culture*. Lanham, Maryland: Hamilton Books, 2010.

Lewis, David Levering. *W.E.B. Du Bois: A Biography*. New York: H. Holt, 2009.

Lindsey, Treva B. *Colored No More: Reinventing Black Womanhood in Washington, D.C.* Urbana: University of Illinois Press, 2017.

Locke, Alain. *The New Negro*. New York: Atheneum, 1992.

Lorde, Audre. "The Uses of the Erotic." In *Sister Outsider: Essays and Speeches*. Trumansburg, NY: Crossing Press, 1984.

Mabley, Jackie. "The Best of Moms Mabley and Pigmeat." *YouTube* video, 36:50. September 23, 2020. https://www.youtube.com/watch?v =YpJtdfQorKw.

———. "Don't Sit on my Bed." *YouTube* video, 4:43. May 29, 2018. https://www.youtube.com/watch?v=4hot_teqE_E.

———. "Moms Mabley: Interview." *YouTube* video, 5:20. October 18, 2011. https://www.youtube.com/watch?v=PWW-96BouIU.

———. "Moms Mabley: Live at Sing Sing." *YouTube* video, 1:05:29. September 25, 2016. https://www.youtube.com/watch?v=as9olj8QHIU.

McDowell, Deborah E. *"The Changing Same": Black Women's Literature, Criticism, and Theory*. Bloomington: Indiana University Press, 1995.

McKee, Margaret, and Fred Chisenhall. *Beale Black & Blue: Life and Music on Black America's Main Street*. Baton Rouge: Louisiana State University Press, 1993.

Micheaux, Oscar, dir. "Swing! (1938)." *YouTube* video, 1:01:13. December 18, 2011. https://www.youtube.com/watch?v=kjrd2C3f6Yo.

Miller, W. Jason. *Langston Hughes*. London: Reaktion Books, 2020.

Mitchell, Michele. "Silences Broken, Silences Kept: Gender and Sexuality in African-American History." *Gender History* 11, no. 3 (November 1999): 433–44. https://doi.org/10.1111/1468-0424.00154.

Monroe, Barbara. "Courtship, Comedy, and African-American Expressive Culture in Zora Neale Hurston's Fiction." In *Look Who's Laughing: Gender and Comedy*, edited by Gail Finney, 173–88. Davis: University of California, 1994.

Morgan, Joan. "Why We Get Off: Moving towards a Black Feminist Politics of Pleasure." *Black Scholar* 45, no. 4 (October 2, 2015): 36–46. https://doi.org/10.1080/00064246.2015.1080915.

Nash, Jennifer C. *The Black Body in Ecstasy: Reading Race, Reading Pornography*. Durham, NC: Duke University Press, 2014.

Nassour, Ellis. "Moms Mabley." In *Harlem Renaissance Lives from the African American National Biography*, edited by Henry Louis Gates and Evelyn Brooks Higginbotham. Oxford University Press, 2009.

Nelson, William E. "Criminality and Sexual Morality in New York, 1920–1980." *Yale Journal of Law and the Humanities* 5 (January 1993). https://doi.org/https://digitalcommons.law.yale.edu/cgi/viewcontent.cgi?article=1091&context=yjlh.

Nylan, Michael. "Lots of Pleasure but Little Happiness." *Philosophy East and West* 65, no. 1 (2015): 196–226. https://doi.org/10.1353/pew.2015.0000.

Oakley, Giles. *The Devil's Music: A History of the Blues*. New York: Da Capo Press, 1997.

Ogbar, Jeffrey. *The Harlem Renaissance Revisited: Politics, Arts, and Letters*. Baltimore, MD: Johns Hopkins University Press, 2010.

Oxford Lexico, s.v. "pleasure." Accessed February 8, 2021. https://www.lexico.com/en/definition/pleasure.

Pauley, Garth E. "W.E.B. Du Bois on Woman Suffrage." *Journal of Black Studies* 30, no. 3 (January 2000): 383–410. https://doi.org/10.1177/002193470003000306.

Peterson, Bernard L. *Profiles of African American Stage Performers and Theatre People, 1816–1960*. Westport, CT: Greenwood Press, 2001.

Pullen, Kirsten. *Like a Natural Woman: Spectacular Female Performance in Classical Hollywood*. London: Rutgers University Press, 2014.

Russell, Thaddeus. "The Color of Discipline: Civil Rights and Black Sexuality." *American Quarterly* 60, no. 1 (2008): 101–28. https://doi.org/10.1353/aq.2008.0000.

Sharpley-Whiting, Denean T. *Bricktop's Paris: African American Women in Paris between the Two World Wars*. Albany: State University of New York Press, 2015.

Sotiropoulos, Karen. *Staging Race: Black Performers in Turn of the Century America*. Cambridge, MA: Harvard University Press, 2006.

Stallings, L. H. *Mutha' Is Half a Word: Intersections of Folklore, Vernacular, Myth, and Queerness in Black Female . . . Culture*. Columbus: Ohio State University Press, 2007.

Tate, Claudia. *Psychoanalysis and Black Novels: Desire and the Protocols of Race*. New York: Oxford University Press, 1998.

Thompson, Marcy. "Picturing the Past: Railroad Dramatically Boosted Brevard's Population." *Transylvania Times*. August 24, 2018.

Tribbett, Marcus Charles. "'Everybody Wants to Buy My Kitty': Resistance and the Articulation of the Sexual Subject in the Blues of Memphis Minnie." *Arkansas Review: Journal of Delta Studies* 29 (April 1998): 42–54.

Tucker, Terrence T. *Furiously Funny: Comic Rage from Ralph Ellison to Chris Rock*. Gainesville: University Press of Florida, 2017.

Wall, Cheryl A. *Worrying the Line: Black Women Writers, Lineage, and Literary Tradition*. Chapel Hill: University of North Carolina Press, 2005.

Wasserman, Jerry. "Queen Bee, King Bee: The Color Purple and the Blues." *Canadian Review of American Studies* 30, no. 3 (January 2000): 300–17. https://doi.org/10.3138/cras-s030-03-03.

Weisenfeld, Judith. "'The Secret at the Root': Performing African American Religious Modernity in Hall Johnson's Run, Little Chillun." *Religion and American Culture: Journal of Interpretation* 21, no. 1 (2011): 39–79. https://doi.org/10.1525/rac.2011.21.1.39.

Welcome, Alexander H. "Our Bodies for Ourselves: Lithe Phenomenal Bodies in the Stand-up of Jackie 'Moms' Mabley." *Black Women, Gender & Families* 4, no. 1 (2010): 87–107. https://doi.org/10.1353/bwg.0.0019.

Williams, Carmaletta M., and John Edgar Tidwell, eds. *My Dear Boy: Carrie Hughes's Letters to Langston Hughes, 1926–1938.* Athens: University of Georgia Press, 2013.

Williams, Elsie A. *The Humor of Jackie Moms Mabley: An African American Comedic Tradition.* n.p.: Routledge, 1995.

Wilson, James. *Bulldaggers, Pansies, and Chocolate Babies Performance, Race, and Sexuality in the Harlem Renaissance.* Ann Arbor: University of Michigan Press, 2010.

Wright, Richard. "Between Laughter and Tears." *New Masses*, October 5, 1937.

Yancy, George. *Black Bodies, White Gazes: The Continuing Significance of Race in America.* Lanham, MD: Rowman & Littlefield Publishers, 2008.

Index

About the Author

TARA T. GREEN is professor and former director of African American and African Diaspora Studies at the University of North Carolina in Greensboro. She is the author of two books, *A Fatherless Child: Autobiographical Perspectives of African American Men*, winner of the 2011 Outstanding Scholarship in Africana Studies Award from the National Council for Black Studies, and *Reimagining the Middle Passage: Black Resistance in Literature, Television, and Song*. She is also the editor of *From the Plantation to the Prison: African-American Confinement Literature* and *Presenting Oprah Winfrey, Her Films, and African American Literature*. Inspired by her upbringing in the New Orleans area, she has completed a literary biography on the life and work of Alice Dunbar-Nelson.